FOREX TRADING

THE ESSENTIAL GUIDE

TO APPROACH FOREX PROFESSIONALLY

John Atkins

Table of Contents

Introduction

The following chapters will discuss the important steps and information a beginner should take and heed to if he or she wants to succeed in Forex Trading.

The first chapter is an introduction to Forex Trading, and it goes into the definition of Forex, and lists down the principles of forex trading. Furthermore, the chapter goes into detail to explain the different types of forex traders, the advantages an individual would enjoy by becoming a forex trader, and reasons an individual should choose forex trading over other forms of trading.

The second chapter dives into the basics of forex trading, and it begins with the definition of important terminologies and trades. The chapter provides an in-depth explanation of forex markets, currency pair basics, and concludes with quote currency. The third chapter is a guide for beginners on the things they need to do to become forex traders. The chapter begins with an explanation of the role of a foreign exchange broker, the importance of a considerable account balance, and the various tools and platforms a forex trader should make use of.

The fourth chapter is an in-depth study of Forex Trading technical analysis and fundamental analysis, and in addition to the value, they offer a forex trader. The fifth chapter is about the mindset a forex trader needs to develop, since such an individual must develop a form of discipline and way of thinking that the direction of the markets will not influence easily. The chapter discusses the attitude approach and the personality types traders have.

The sixth chapter is a study of the different strategies forex traders can implement in their business to become successful. The chapter begins with an explanation of the most popular and effective strategies traders use and then concludes with the most appropriate strategies for beginners.

The seventh chapter is about the various Forex Trading signals, and it begins with an explanation of the signals. The chapter continues to explain the most popular signals traders use out there and how they work, both the manual and automated forex trading signals. The chapter concludes with a guide to choosing the best signals and evaluating the free forex signals option.

The eighth chapter is a valuable resource on the tips an individual would need to follow to start winning in Forex Trading. The chapter explains the different tips and best kept secrets, and it concludes with the strategies a trader can implement to manage risks. The ninth chapter is about cryptocurrencies and the value they can have on a forex trader's business strategies.

The tenth chapter offers three forex trading examples that a beginner would look at to have even more insights into this business. The eleventh chapter is an explanation into the mistakes Forex Traders make, and the preventive measures, as well as solutions a new trader should look into to have better chances of success.

The final chapter is about making money as a forex trader. The chapter explains how forex signals, forex robots, and social trading can help a beginner to make the most out of every trade.

There are plenty of books on this subject on the market, thanks again for choosing this one! Every effort was made to ensure it is full of as much useful information as possible, please enjoy!

Chapter 1: An Introduction to Forex Trading

If you have been to a foreign country, you know that you cannot buy your favorite food and drinks in the country you are visiting with your home country's currency. To avoid such a predicament, individuals have the option to convert their money into the currency of the country they are visiting at the airport.

In addition, you may have received some payment for services in a foreign currency, and you needed to exchange the money into your country's currency for you to use it. Regardless of the situations you had interacting with foreign currency. It is likely highly you have participated in forex in one way or another. A person can participate in Forex Trading whether he or she is traveling to a foreign country, or doing business in his or her country.

What Is Forex Trading

The word 'forex' is short for 'foreign exchange.' It involves the process of converting one currency into another currency for reasons including tourism, trading, and business.

Although a person can participate in foreign exchange by traveling to a different country and exchanging his or her currency for the foreign country's currency, the foreign exchange market is more significant than that. The foreign exchange market is a global forum for exchanging substantial national currencies against each other.

Due to the international spread of finance and trade, the forex markets experience high demands for foreign currencies, which makes the market the most significant money market in the world.

When multinational companies intend to buy goods from other countries, companies need to find the local currency first. That exchange will involve vast amounts of currency exchange. As a result, the local currency value will move up as the demand for that currency increases. With that exchanging going on around the world, the exchange rate always changes.

When global traders exchange currencies, currencies have a specific exchange rate, the price of currency changes according to the law of supply and demand; the higher the demand, the higher the supply and the higher the exchange rate.

The foreign trading market has no centralized marketplace for foreign exchange. Foreign exchange bureaus operate electronically through computer networks between traders all over the world.

Therefore, foreign trading goes on for 24 hours a day, six days a week in leading financial centers of major capital cities around the world. Investment and commercial banks carry out most of the Forex Trading in the international marketplaces in place of clients and investors.

Principles of Forex Trading

1. Learn the Market's Trends

It is essential for one to be able to predict the changing nature of the foreign exchange market in order to be successful in Forex Trading.

Accordingly, a person should understand the general direction of the marketplace. Trends can be uptrend, downtrend, or sideways trend. Identifying a pattern can profit a person in that he or she will be able to trade with the trend.

Uptrends are trends that move upwards, indicating an appreciation in currency value. Downtrends move downwards as an indication of depreciation in currency value. Sideways trends show that the currencies are neither appreciating nor depreciating.

2. Stay Focused and Control Your Emotions

Forex Trading is a challenging marketplace that can cause a person to lose confidence and to give up in the toughest of times. That is understandable given that traders put in their hard-earned money.

As a result, when a person experiences loss, he or she can lose focus when negative emotions become overwhelming. Some of the negative emotions a person may experience include panic, frustration, depression, and desperation.

It is, therefore, essential for one to become aware of the negative emotions that result from Forex Trading so that he or she may minimize the emotional effects of loss and remain focused.

3. Learn Risk Mitigation Tactics

In order to achieve the profits that a person anticipates, the person needs to minimize the likelihood of financial loss.

Since the forex market keeps on changing, the risks, therefore, keep on changing. The most crucial risk management rule is that a person should not risk more than he or she can afford to lose. Traders who are willing to invest more than they make, become very susceptible to Forex Trading risks.

Consequently, a person can mitigate potential losses by placing stop-loss orders, exchanging more than one currency pair, using software programs for help, and limiting the use of financial leverage.

4. Establish Personal Forex Trading Limits

A person should know when to stop Forex Trading. One can stop Forex Trading when he or she has an unproductive trading plan, or when he or she is continually experiencing losses.

An ineffective Forex Trading plan may not bring trade to an end, but it will not function as well as a trader may expect. In that case, the trader can consider stopping the trade, constantly changing markets, and the decreasing volatility within a particular foreign trading tool may also cause a trader to take a break from Forex Trading.

In addition, when a person is not in a good physical or emotional state, he or she may want to think about taking a break to deal with personal issues.

5. Use Technology to Your Benefit

Being up-to-date with existing technological developments can be gratifying in Forex Trading.

Given that forex markets utilize the online forum, high-speed internet connections can increase Forex Trading performance significantly. In order to make the most of Forex Trading, a person must take it as a full-time occupation, and he or she must embrace new technologies. Similarly, receiving forex market current information with smartphones makes it possible for forex traders to track trades anywhere.

Forex Trading is an aggressive enterprise that needs a trader to have an equally competitive edge. Therefore, a forex trader needs to maximize his or her business's potential by taking full advantage of the available technology.

6. Make Use of a Forex Trading Plan

A Forex Trading plan comprises of rules and guidelines that stipulate a forex trader's entry, exit, and money management principles.

A trading plan provides the opportunity for a forex trader to try out a Forex Trading idea before the trader risks real money. In so doing, a trader can access historical information that helps to know whether a Forex Trading plan is feasible and what outcomes he or she can expect.

When a forex trader comes up with a Forex Trading plan that shows potentially favorable outcomes, he or she can use the trading plan in real Forex Trading situations. The idea is for the forex trader to adhere to the trading plan.

Buying or selling currencies outside of the Forex Trading plans, even if a trader makes a profit, is poor trading, which can end any expectation the plan may have had.

Different Types of Forex Traders

Because foreign markets become flooded with the constant demand for currency exchange, four types of currency traders facilitate the smooth operation of forex markets.

1. Scalpers

Forex scalpers are dealers who buy or sell currencies, hold on to the exchanged currencies, and then wait for them to have higher and favorable exchange rates before the dealers can change their new currencies back to their original versions.

The scalpers hold deals for seconds to minutes and open and close several positions within a single day. In other words, scalpers go in and out of positions several times each day.

Scalpers trade currencies based on real-time analysis. Scalpers aim to make a profit by selling or buying currencies and holding on to them for a short time before buying or selling the currencies back to the forex market for small gains.

Therefore, that means that scalpers should love sitting in front of their laptops or computers for the entire forex session without taking their eyes off the screen.

Scalping is widespread moments after essential data releases and interest rate announcements. That is because high-impact reports generate significant price moves within a short period.

However, while profits can accrue rapidly with profitable trades, huge losses can also accumulate if the scalper is using a faulty system or if the trader does not understand what he or she is doing.

2. Day Traders

Forex day traders control trading positions during each trading day. Day traders close the trading positions at the end of the trading day and ensure that there are no positions that remain open during the night.

Forex day traders use currency day trading systems that regulate whether to buy or sell a currency pair in the foreign exchange market. A currency pair is the quotation of two different currencies where the trader quotes the value of one currency in comparison to the other.

Day traders target day currencies that are very liquid to leverage their capital as soon as investment prices change in favorable directions. The traders pick a price position at the start of the day, act on their assessments, and finish the trading day with either a profit or a loss.

Forex day traders avoid holding positions overnight because that may result in stock price gaps, a consequence, which can be very costly.

3. Swing Traders

Swing traders take hold of a position over a few days to several weeks. They hold places for more than one trading session, although not longer than several weeks or a couple of months.

Swing traders aim to capture huge potential price moves. Some swing traders may look for volatile stocks with constant movements, whereas others prefer stock prices that are more predictable.

Swing traders have exposure to overnight and weekend risks, where prices could rift and open the following forex session with markedly different rates. However, swing traders can generate profit by using established risk or reward strategies that will help them to determine where they will enter assets, where they will place stop-loss orders, and to know where they can make profits. Stop-loss orders help to limit the loss when stock prices fall.

Swing traders come up with plans and strategies that will give them an advantage over may trades. The traders do that by looking for trade arrangements that facilitate predictable price movements in the price of the asset. However, no trade arrangement works every time.

4. Position Traders

Position traders hold on to investment positions for long periods, anticipating the investments to appreciate. The periods can extend from weeks to months. In that regard, position traders are less concerned with short-term changes in price movements.

Position traders follow trends, believing that once a pattern starts, it is likely to continue. As such, position traders incline toward obtaining the bulk of a trend's move, which would generate profit in their investment capital.

Position traders use both fundamental and technical analysis to help in making trading decisions. They also depend on macroeconomic influences, old trends, and overall market movements to get to their anticipated end.

For a trader to have success in position trading, the trader has to know the entry or exit points and have a strategy to mitigate risk mainly by placing stop-loss orders.

Advantage of Forex Trading

1. Easy to Modify

Forex Trading markets put no restrictions on how much money a forex trader can use. Forex traders can trade a variety of goods and services.

In addition, the forex market does not have many rules and regulations for the forex trader to follow. The regulations that exist guide forex traders on when to enter and when to exit a trade.

2. Individual Control

Nobody controls the foreign market. Therefore, a forex trader has complete autonomy concerning making a trade. The forex market regulates itself and levels the playing field.

There are no intermediaries involved – a forex trader trades directly in the open forex market, and a retail forex broker eases that process.

3. Lucidity of Information

The Forex Trading market gives information straightforwardly to the public about the rates and price movement forecasts. The forex market traders have free and equal access to the market's information, and that makes it easy for the traders to make calculated and risk-free trading decisions.

Forex traders also have access to past information that helps in analyzing the market tendencies and forecasting the direction, which the market will take.

4. Widespread Options

The forex market provides a variety of options to forex investors. As a result, forex investors can take advantage of the available options to trade in different currencies in pairs.

An investor has the option of getting into foreign exchange spot trade or trading in currency futures to make the most of his or her investment.

5. High Liquidity and Volume

The forex market trades in large amounts of currencies at any given time because of how active the foreign exchange is. Therefore, there are high chances for forex traders to trade currency pairs on demand.

Under normal market conditions, a forex trader can buy and sell quickly with the anticipation that there will be another forex trader on the other end who is willing to trade back.

6. Money-Making Gains

The forex market provides Forex Trading measures that guard against financial loss. To ensure that a forex trader maximizes of gaining profits, the forex market has provisions for minimizing loss through making stop-loss orders.

Stop-loss orders enable forex traders to determine the closing price of their trade and thereby avoiding unforeseen losses.

7. 24-Hour Market

Foreign exchange markets remain open for 24-hours a day and 6 days a week. That means that the market stays open most of the time, and it is not subject to external factors that may affect it.

Consequently, forex traders are flexible to work during the hours that suit them best.

8. Low Operation Costs

Operation costs in the forex currency markets are competent in trading in the forex market. The cost of operation in the currency market is in the form of spreads measured in pips. A pip is the fourth place after the decimal point of a percent.

For example, is the selling price was 2.5887, and the buying price was 2.5889, then the transaction cost is 2pips. Brokers may charge commissions on a fraction of the amount of the trade.

9. Chief Financial Market

The forex market is the biggest financial market in the world. That is because global corporations and big financial institutions participate dynamically in the foreign exchange market.

The foreign exchange market empowers major financial institutions to retail stockholders to seek out profits from currency variations connected to the global economy.

10.   One Can Use the Leverage

The forex markets allow forex traders to capitalize on the advantage. Leveraging enables forex traders to be able to open positions for thousands of dollars while investing small amounts of money.

For example, when a forex trader trades at 40:1 leverage, he or she can trade $40 for every $1 that was in his or her account. That means that the forex trader can manage a trade of $40,000 for every $1,000 of investment.

Why Forex

The foreign exchange market is open to all types of traders, and it is more accessible than any other online trading platform in the world. Similarly, one can start trading with as little as $100. Therefore, foreign exchange markets have lower exchange capital prerequisites compared to other financial markets. A person can quickly sign up to open their trading account online, where most forex retail brokers operate.

Forex Trading is easy to learn, although it may be challenging to master. However, once an investor understands how the forex market works, he or she will be open to a world of vast opportunities that include becoming a foreign exchange account manager. A foreign exchange account manager can accumulate profits from trading as well as earning commissions for managing the Forex Trading accounts.

Foreign exchange markets make provisions for forex brokers to develop considerable trading volumes because of the leverage that the forex markets offer. That explains why forex traded get rewards like deposit bonuses when creating a Forex Trading account. Likewise, forex brokers give several incentives and promotions to financial institutions that enter Forex Trading. As a result, the forex market becomes a stimulating marketplace for Forex Trading.

Forex traders form international social communities as more people sign up every day. The social networks help forex investors to encounter an entire community of foreign exchange traders, thus making the forex market an interactive market to trade. In addition, forex traders can find many international forex experts, contributors, critics, and educators, among other members, in every conceivable language.

Moreover, forex traders can buy and sell risk-free, using a demonstration trading account. The account prevents traders from putting their investment at risk, and the traders can, therefore, move to the live forex markets whenever they please. The trading accounts enable forex traders to have access to real-time market information and the latest trading wisdom from foreign experts.

The forex market infrastructure is sophisticated, causing the performance of traders to be even more level. The forex market also has low spreads and commissions, thus making the transaction costs relatively small as a result. Besides, the foreign exchange market educates forex traders on global events, as the traders continue to trade online. Favorable trading conditions are crucial for foreign exchange traders.

Heavy security measures guard the foreign exchange markets, and several authorities control every forex broker. The bodies exist to make sure that forex traders have a safe space to carry out Forex Trading activities. However, forex traders are only with regulated brokers. Therefore, one must conduct a background check on available brokers in order to ensure that he or she works with the regulated brokers.

Online Forex Trading makes use of advanced trading software that generates regular updates that help forex investors to make real-time Forex Trading decisions. Consequently, Forex Trading becomes a rewarding way to buy and sell online, also due to third-party software developers who provide add-ons and plugins for popular trading platforms.

Finally, the forex markets allow traders to buy low and sell high. What's more, forex traders can trade assets without owning them, a practice that is called short selling. Furthermore, the use of leverage enables Forex traders to buy or sell more substantial amounts than what they have in their deposits.

Chapter 2: Basics of Forex Trading

The term Forex Trading stands for foreign exchange trading, which is the purchasing or selling of one type of currency in exchange for another one. Also known as FX, it is a global over-the-counter market where investors, traders, banks, and institutions speculate on, purchase, and sell world currencies.

Forex Trading happens over the interbank market, which is a channel through which currency trading happens 5 days a week, 24 hours a day. It is one of the biggest trading markets in the world, with a worldwide daily turnover estimated to be more than $5 trillion. This is because countries, businesses, and individuals all participate in Forex Trading.

Actually, when people visit another country and convert their currency to the local currency, they are participating in the FX market. The demand for a particular currency at any given time will either push its value up or down in relation to other currencies. Therefore, people who want to venture into Forex Trading should understand a few important things before making their first trade, including:

1. Learning about currency pairs and what they mean

2. Market pricing

Forex transactions involve the simultaneous buying and selling of two different currencies known as currency pairs, which include a quote currency and a base currency. One of the most popular currency pairs on the forex market is the Euro/US Dollar. Also called the counter currency, the quote currency is the second currency in a forex pair.

Forex prices often have four decimal places due to their very small spread differences. However, they can also have any number of decimal places. Trades on the forex market are often worth millions of dollars; therefore, even tiny price differences can add up to a significant profit.

However, such massive trading volumes mean that a small spread can also lead to significant losses. Therefore, forex traders should consider the risks involved and trade carefully.

Important Terminology and Trades

A position, in terms of Forex Trading, describes a trade in progress. A long position, for instance, means that a forex trader purchased currency expecting its value to go up. Once he/she sells it back to the market at a higher price, the trade is complete, and his/her long position closes.

A short position, on the other hand, refers to a situation where a trader sells a certain currency with the expectation that its value will decrease, with the aim of buying it back at a lower price. The short position will close once the trader buys back the currency, ideally at a lower price.

If the currency pair of EUR/USD, which refers to Euro/US Dollar, was trading at 1.0914/1.0916, for example, investors planning to open a long position on the Euro would purchase one Euro for 1.0916 US dollars. They will then hold on to the currency and hope that its value will increase, and then sell it back to the market once it appreciates.

On the other hand, investors looking to open a short position on the Euro will sell one Euro for 1.0914 US dollars, with the expectation that its value will depreciate. If their expectations come true, they will buy it back at the lower rate and make a profit.

Forex Markets

With central banks, retail forex brokers, commercial corporations, commercial banks, hedge funds, individual investors, and investment management firms participating in the forex market, it is easy to see why this market is larger than equity and futures markets combined.

Placing a trade in the forex market is quite simple. The basics of Forex Trading are very similar to the mechanics of other financial markets, such as the stock market. Therefore, traders with prior experience in any type of financial market should be able to understand Forex Trading quite quickly.

1. Basics of the Forex Market

The FX market is a global network of brokers and computers from around the world; therefore, no single market exchange dominates this market. These brokers are also market makers and often post bid and ask prices for currency pairs, which are often different from the most competitive bid in the FX market.

On a more basic level, the foreign exchange market consists of two levels, i.e., the over-the-counter market and the interbank market. The OTC market is where individual traders execute trades through brokers and online platforms. The interbank market, on the other hand, is where large banking institutions trade currencies on behalf of clients or for purposes of balance sheet adjustments and hedging.

2. Hours of Operation

The FX market is a 24-hour market, from Monday morning to Friday afternoon in Asia and New York, respectively. Essentially, unlike markets such as commodities, bonds, and equities that close for a while, the forex market does not close even at night. However, there are exceptions. Some currencies for emerging markets, for example, close for a short while during the trading day.

3. The Currency Giants

By far, the US dollar is the biggest player in Forex Trading, making up approximately 85% of all forex trades. The second most traded currency is the euro, which makes up close to 39% of all currency trades, while the Japanese yen comes in at third place with 19% of all currency trades.

The reason that these figures do not total 100% is that every forex transaction involves two currencies. Citigroup and JPMorgan Chase and Co. were the biggest participants in the FX market in 2018, according to a study conducted by Greenwich Associates. Actually, these two banks commanded more than 30% of the global forex market share.

Goldman Sachs, Deutsche Bank, and UBS made up the remaining top five places. According to a settlement and processing group known as CLS, the daily trading volume in January last year was more than $1.8 trillion. This is a testament to just how popular, and massive Forex Trading is around the world.

4. Origins of the Forex Market

Up until the First World War, countries based their currencies on precious metals like silver and gold. This system, however, collapsed, and the Bretton Woods agreement became the basis of currencies after the Second World War. This agreement led to the creation of three international organizations to oversee economic activities across the world.

These organizations were the General Agreement on Tariffs and Trade, the International Monetary Fund, and the International Bank for Reconstruction and Development. In addition to creating these international organizations, the agreement adopted the US dollar as the peg for international currencies, instead of gold.

In return, the US government had to back up dollar supplies with an equivalent amount or value of gold reserves. This system, however, ended in 1971 when Richard Nixon, the US president at the time, suspended the US dollar's convertibility into gold. Nowadays, currencies can pick their own peg, and the forces of demand and supply determine their value.

Currency Pairs and Their Prices

These are quotations of two different currencies, such as EUR/USD. They quote the value of the first currency, which is the base currency, against the second one, which is the quote currency. Essentially, a currency pair compares the value of the first currency against the second one, showing how much the first/quote currency can but one unit of the second/base currency.

An ISO currency code identifies currencies. This is the 3-letter alphabetic code, such as EUR for the euro, associated with a particular currency on the international market. When traders place an order for a currency pair, it means that they are purchasing the base currency and selling the quote currency. According to FX trading statistics, the most liquid currency pair in the world is the EUR/USD, followed by the USD/JPY.

1. Currency Pair Basics

Forex Trading happens in the foreign exchange market, which is the most liquid and largest market in the financial arena. Although it involves the simultaneous sale of one currency and purchase of another, forex traders should think of a currency pair as a single unit to purchase or sell.

Essentially, when a forex trader purchases a currency pair, he/she buys the base currency and, in effect, sells the second/quoted currency. The buy/bid price represents how much of the quote currency he/she will need to purchase one unit of the base currency.

On the other hand, when the trader sells a currency pair, he/she is selling the base currency and implicitly getting the quote currency. In this case, the sell/ask price for the currency pair will represent how much he/she will receive in terms of the quote currency for selling a single unit of the base currency.

2. Major Currency Pairs

There are numerous currencies in the world, which means that there are just as many currency pairs. Currencies come and go; therefore, the total number of currency pairs tends to change. However, investors categorize currency pairs based on their daily trading volume. Those that trade the most against the USD are the major currencies, and these include:

1. EUR/USD
2. USD/CHF
3. USD/JPY
4. USD/CAD
5. GBP/USD
6. AUD/USD

These major currency pairs account for almost 80% of the global Forex trading volume. They usually have high liquidity and low volatility and are indicative of well-managed and stable economies. In addition, they have narrower spreads than other currency pairs and are less susceptible to currency manipulation strategies.

3. Cross Currency Pairs

Also called crosses, these currency pairs do not include the US dollar. A few years ago, investors looking to trade crosses first had to convert them into the US dollar and then into the currency they desired. However, nowadays, investors can make direct cross currency pairs exchanges.

The most popular crosses feature minor currency pairs, such as GBP/JPY, EUR/JPY, and EUR/GBP. Cross-currency pairs are usually more volatile and less liquid than major currency pairs.

4. Exotic Pairs

These consist of currencies from smaller or emerging economies, paired with a major currency. Compared to two types of currency pairs discussed above, trading in exotics involves higher risk because they are significantly volatile and less liquid, which means they are more susceptible to currency manipulation.

Exotics also have wider spreads and are extremely sensitive to certain financial developments and unexpected changes in the political climate.

Quote Currency

Commonly referred to as the counter currency, the quote currency is the second one in both an indirect and direct currency pair. The quote currency determines the value of the base currency. In an indirect quote, the domestic currency is the quote currency, while the foreign currency is the quote currency in a direct quote.

The value of the quote currency falls as the rate in the currency pair goes up. This is the case irrespective of whether the pair is indirect or direct. It is important for forex traders to understand the pricing structure and quotation of currencies in the FX market. Forex brokers tend to trade certain currency pairs in specific ways.

Therefore, understanding the fundamentals of the quote currency is an important step towards finding success in Forex Trading. The exchange rate of a currency pair shows how much of the quote currency traders need to buy or sell to sell or buy one unit of the base currency. The value of the quote currency will be decreasing as the currency pair's rate increases, whether it is indirect or direct.

USD/CAD, for example, is a direct quote that denotes the cross-rate between the US dollar and the Canadian dollar, which is the quote currency in this case, while the US dollar is the base currency. Therefore, investors will use the Canadian dollar as a reference to determine the US dollar's value. From a US perspective, the Canadian dollar is a foreign currency.

The EUR/USD currency pair, on the other hand, describes the cross-rate between the euro and the US dollar; however, it is an indirect quote. In other words, the US dollar is the quote currency, and the euro is the base currency. In this case, the US dollar is the domestic currency that determines the value of a single unit of the euro.

The investment market can easily relieve investors of their money if they fail to prepare themselves well or adhere to the fundamental principles of trading. In any investment market, trading can be exceedingly tricky and difficult. However, success comes with adequate practice and education, and anyone with the right mindset can succeed at Forex Trading.

Learning about foreign exchange trading is the first thing that prospective forex traders should focus on. There are tons of learning materials and tools available to both experienced and new forex traders. It is also important to work with a regulated broker with several years of experience.

Chapter 3: How to Get Started in Forex Trading

Who Is A Foreign Exchange Broker?

Brokers are the intermediaries who link investors with their capital. Some traders may choose to invest in the forex trade, and therefore they will invariably become in need of a foreign exchange broker. Forex is a shortened version of the term Foreign Exchange. This phrase represents the financial market site within which various trading processes, deals, and transactions in foreign currency take place. Based on this description, a foreign exchange broker is, therefore, a registered and more qualified expert in currency trading.

Such forex brokers offer their services to prospective investors in foreign exchange and other currency traders who may require specific complex services. They identify opportunities, execute complicated trading strategies, and manage financial risk exposure on your behalf. Hence, a foreign exchange broker will assist you in achieving your aims of making a significant profit and mitigate potential losses. He or she is responsible for guiding you on how to manage your investment capital in the currency market.

Those brokers who deal in foreign exchange services typically know when and how to react or respond to volatility within the financial market. They provide the support mechanism that enables you to navigate through the uncertainty associated with currency trading successfully. In addition, such forex brokers often have extensive experience as previous traders in the forex markets. Therefore, you should always heed their advice and pay attention to their guidance or occasional recommendations.

Most forex brokers, upon hiring, will come with various trading platforms and accompanying tools to assist you in proper forex investment. Management of your available capital and exposure to risk may be your responsibility, but the advice of a forex broker is equally essential. The currency trading tools and relevant software platforms vary in their specific applications and features. Forex brokers will also make sure to teach you about the extensive range of traders and expertise required to master each of the separate platforms.

For you to understand the data and information contained in Forex Trading tools, you need to learn particular skills in technical analysis. This analytical expertise is transferable from the forex brokers to prospective traders and new investors through learning. You can grasp some knowledge of how to perform and correctly interpret the various forms of foreign exchange technical analyses. The associated foreign exchange terminology is relevant to know, as well. The foreign exchange broker can bring your attention to any other currency investment opportunities that may be available in the financial market.

Besides, the forex broker can distinguish the productive and probably profitable currency deals from the doomed ones. Due to the lax regulations in the currency market, you should beware of fraudulent brokers. You need to be highly suspicious of those brokers who claim to specialize in foreign exchange per se. whenever you encounter such seemingly dedicated brokers, you should sever ties with them instantly. You should engage a general stockbroker who has an additional registration in Forex Trading. Besides, it is rare to find phony stockbrokers due to the stringent regulation of the stock markets and stock exchanges. Select a well-known brokerage firm to have a chance of success in trading currencies.

The foreign exchange is the largest financial market in the world currently, and it is the most liquid kind of all the available markets too. Daily, it can experience currency exchanges to the tune of trillions. You will need the guidance of a foreign exchange broker to participate in this market, especially if you are new to the concept of currency trading. With the advent of the World Wide Web, this market has had an exclusive electronic presence online.

The internet connects the various stakeholders involved in Forex Trading, such as financial institutions, private investors, retail traders, and foreign exchange brokers. Since it is an online entity, the forex market is always active throughout the day. Whenever you want to participate in the currency trade, you need to interact with the other currency queries in the market. This interaction is possible by posting relevant orders online for you to engage in either buying or selling currencies or even conduct both.

When you are new to foreign exchange, you can begin investing in retail trading. Here, profits and losses are simply the difference between your buying and selling prices of the relevant currencies. When buying currency, you will hope for a rise in its value over the allocated trading time frame. The opposite is exact of a situation involving selling money, and therefore, these two scenarios are the distinct routes to making a profit in cases of simple retail trading.

You may experience motivation for a change in the currency price. Hence, you are more likely to roll over your positions on most days. Rollover positions attract a commission or fees depending on the kind of forex broker that you use. However, this charge and other brokerage costs get an automatic credit or debit to your forex account.

Spot transactions describe the types of trade deals that ensure immediate resolution without the need for a rollover. Such trades are especially useful for people who are sensitive to nagging costs, charges, and fees. Only the presence of holidays can render spot trade deals impossible and hence the need for its postponement. Another way to interact in foreign exchange involves speculating on the future value of a particular currency relative to a different one.

This activity needs your correct predictive skills in the future exchange rate between a pair of specific currencies. Speculation is a tactic that is relevant to futures and forwards in the forex market. These two types of Forex Trading differ in their customizability after the expiry of a specified trading period. It is possible to customize the forwards with the currency under trade. The possibility maintains even after the lapse of the trading time interval. The futures, however, are not as customizable as forwards, and in fact, they do not permit it. Therefore, a foreign exchange broker would advise you on how to proceed with these situations.

As earlier mentioned, spot transactions are usual in retail trading, while currency forwards and futures involve trading with some degree of speculation. You will need to deal in futures contracts when making predictions in the currency market. Its principle is similar to options trading whereby you begin by purchasing a currency futures contract.

Next, you should take a particular position on the future behavior of a specific currency relative to another different type of currency. Your contract becomes due for settlement upon the expiry of your allocated trading period. However, currency futures do not allow for any further negotiations past the expiry period. This strictness is unlike the situation with bespoke forward contracts that would enable settlement at any time. Besides, you should close your futures contract trading position before the expiration date to avoid additional settlement costs. Just like options trading, taking multiple trading positions on the future values of various currencies is possible, as well.

What Is the Account Balance, and Why Does a Broker Need It?

The account balance is the amount of equity or capital available in your brokerage account due to investment in the currency market. It is essential to have such an account to enable the foreign exchange broker to carry out the buying and selling executions on your behalf. Since your investment is in the currency market, this brokerage account is your forex account, as well. Opening a forex account for a new investor is a simple exercise that is akin to opening a personal bank account. After setting up a forex account, you should seek the services of an accomplished and registered forex broker. All foreign exchange trade deals and transactions should go through your forex broker. Therefore, he or she needs to gain access to this forex account and have permission to transact in the currency market on your behalf.

An investor's limited involvement in the daily running of the account necessitates that the forex broker takes over these duties. In addition, other financial liabilities charged to this account include the commissions and brokerage fees. You should check on the forex account regularly to keep track of the progress of your investments.

It also allows you to carry out responsible financial management based on the difference between your finances and risk liabilities. Productive risk management strategies become possible based on the available capital balance in the account at a particular moment. Since the currency market tends to turn volatile without warning, your forex account must maintain its liquidity status. The available balance provides your forex broker with the necessary leeway to take immediate corrective measures when a specific currency trade deal begins to go wrong. The best way to ensure that the brokerage account retains activity is to make regular deposits into it.

A standing order is a useful way of guaranteeing the liquidity status of the forex account. Your order will execute the transfer of a certain sum of money from your private account at regular intervals of your choosing. This automatic process eliminates the downsides associated with forgetfulness on your part. In the case of currency trading that involves derivatives, the forex broker can easily buy and sell futures contracts based on their speculation at a particular time.

Currency fluctuations require your forex broker to take a specific position promptly to take advantage of the time factor in currency trading. Financial delays from an inactive or overdrawn brokerage account are often responsible for some of your indirect losses. As a result, your forex broker will miss out on potentially profitable opportunities in the currency market.

Another importance attributed to the forex account is the possibility of a quick integration with the trading platform and technical analysis tools. Your forex broker will have access to both the forex account and the trading platform in a single place. Hence, making informed decisions becomes an instantaneous activity. The forex broker reacts to data and information from technical analyses with the appropriate monetary input.

This activity may involve either more investment in a promising opportunity or a straightforward exit from a non-productive trade deal. You can easily relate the comparison between any technical analyses performed and the balance available in your forex account. Your forex broker has the freedom to make long-term decisions and speculation only if he or she is sure of the availability of capital. Because of taking such high risks, your forex broker is more likely to make higher profits for you.

In the case of taking long positions on forwards and futures contracts, the forex broker should feel confident in his or her level of liquidity. Confidence breeds more self-belief, and eventually, the forex broker ends up conducting sensible transactions. Emotional reactions to trading positions are typical of forex brokers who are always wary of taking risks due to the fear of losing the scanty balance available. Insufficient capital and account mismanagement typically result in forex brokers who continuously engage in illogical trade deals to cover recent losses. You will find such forex brokers participating in the short-term local currency trading more frequently with your capital.

Further investigation of your forex broker may reveal the underlying cause as the fear of losing your money and, in turn, his or her commission. Always make sure that you are abreast of the condition of your forex account. You can offer appropriate instructions and proper orders on the level of risks that you may tolerate. Such instructions are only possible if you keep track of the activities in the account. In addition, you and your forex broker can plan risk management strategies together to limit your exposure to unnecessary financial risks. The forex broker will grow accustomed to your mannerisms gradually, and soon he or she will understand your objectives. At this point, the forex broker becomes comfortable enough to exert the full range of his or her trading expertise towards the attainment of your financial goals.

What Are Platforms and Tools?

A trading platform is the graphical user interface provided by computer application software, and it enables the trader or investor to interact with the aspects of his or her trading transactions. A Forex Trading platform is a standard provision from most forex brokers to their clients, investors, or other retail traders. It also acts as a source of commission for the forex brokers by charging an access fee to use it. After seeking a foreign exchange broker, most traders will get a couple of trading platform recommendations from these same brokers.

Forex brokers are often adept at their jobs, and hence these recommendations are typically advisable. When you decide to participate in foreign currency trading, you will need to familiarize yourself with the skills of taking profitable market positions. Therefore, you will have to purchase, download, and install the software on your computer and learn to navigate around the online platform.

In case you are new to online Forex Trading, it may become somewhat challenging to make your way around the platform. For you to understand and succeed in this particular endeavor, you will need the assistance of an online foreign exchange broker.

Due to the competition among different foreign exchange brokers, some of the online trading platforms may be available at a discount or even free of charge. It is essential that you know which one will work best for you based on their simplicity of use, precision, and online forex broker support. Most of your investment and capital management decisions depend on your understanding of the forex market. A robust and versatile platform should make it easier for you to come up with informed choices. In addition, an excellent online platform should have an online forex broker standing by for technical analysis and support.

Another aspect concerning Forex Trading platforms is the range of the available versions. They vary from the low end of the trading spectrum to the high end of trading end users. You can have the primary platforms consisting of rudimentary trading user interfaces for the beginners and new investors. Besides, there are sophisticated platforms that contain multiple analytical tools with enhanced graphics and live streaming capability for seasoned traders.

When choosing a relevant platform, you should keep in mind the amount of capital you intend to invest and the level of risk exposure that you can tolerate. The initial cost and the presence of subscription fees are other vital deliberations to make during the selection process as well. All the essential features needed for Forex Trading are common to most platforms; hence, the availability of multiple and excessive aspects is not such a significant consideration when buying one. You can narrow down your choice to the platforms that have the features that you will require only. As an investor, you should make decisions concerning the kind of platforms based on your forex broker's reputation.

Meta Trader is the most famous Forex Trading platform in the market currently. Its development resulted from the use of a versatile programming language that employs scripting as an execution method, i.e., the MQL program. Meta Trader can support multiple types of order executions, allows for simultaneous editing while trading, and can conduct hedging operations. In addition, the platform has an embedded email system, technical indicators, analytical, graphical objects, and the ability to chat online with fellow traders.

Currently, the Meta Trader platform is in its fifth version. Other platforms' primary purposes differ from foreign currency exchanges. However, they often have some level of forex capacity inbuilt within their structure. Examples of these different platforms include the IG group, CMC Markets, X-Trade Brokers, Pepper Stone, Forex.Com, Robin Hood, Trade Station, TDA merit trade, and Interactive Brokers.

On the other hand, foreign exchange trading tools are the indicators that show you how the market and your capital are performing. They are mainly the outcomes of technical analysis conducted on the various trading positions taken in your Forex Trading deals. The presentation of the results of such studies occurs via a graphical user interface that provides relatable information that is easily understandable. Most trading platforms have embedded tools within their structure to provide all the necessary data at one point. This platform flexibility eliminates the need to acquire separate stand-alone tools for each analytical process. The kinds of information derived from currency trading tools are in the form of graphical objects such as tables and charts for reports and analysis, respectively.

Line graphs are specifically standard in trend and pattern analysis. Monitoring currency fluctuations is better using such a graphical representation. Hence, most, if not all, trading tools are akin to the technical, analytical tools that are exclusive to foreign exchange trades. The only slight difference is that they are currently presentable online via computers as opposed to the previous use of paperwork.

The tools that are within the Meta Trader platform provide information on daily market analysis as well as Forex Trading signals on market trends and fluctuations. Consistent capital and risk management strategies are essential deliverables credited to the use of Forex Trading tools. You can adjust your trading position based on the data from these tools. The adjustments may involve reinforcing your stance on a forex position due to the use of a more valuable currency in a favorable market. In addition, you can consider exiting a trade deal altogether when the currency values become too volatile to sustain investor confidence.

Currency converters, economic calendars, financial news streams, and various types of calculators are additional tools available on most Forex Trading platforms. Computation of potential profits and losses within the Meta Trader platform is possible using tools such as profit, pip, margin, and invest-profit calculators. Your financial risk increases with the rise in the volatility of the currency market.

In such a situation, the margin calculator is also responsible for conducting your probable risk assessment. Forex Trading applications that are customizable to your smartphones are another form of tools available to you during trading. These so-called apps are beneficial in that they are portable and enable you to keep track of your financial progress at any time, as well as in real-time. Examples of such mobile forex tools include Coin Trader, FX Trader, Trade Interceptor, Forex Hours, and XE Currency.

Chapter 4: Technical and Fundamental Analysis in Forex Trading

Forex Trading involves a market of an electronic network of brokers, individual traders, institutions, and banks, which trade a variety of national currencies. Excluding a holiday, a forex market opens throughout for five days a week, and it is the liquid and most prominent financial market worldwide. Forex Trading is essential to traders and financial institutions as it offers them profits from the movements of the currency. Technical and fundamental analyses are the two primary methods that a trader can use to study and assess the forex market.

A trader needs to learn and understand how the two forms of analysis work. He or she also should be able to tell the difference that takes place in the application of each analysis type. This knowledge will help him or her to read the market better and even make fitting speculations regarding the direction of specific currency movements. As a result, the trader can take up appropriate positions in the market that will enable him or her to receive gains from the trades.

Below is information that provides a breakdown of how technical and fundamental analysis functions in Forex Trading.

Technical Analysis

Technical analysis is a methodology that a trader uses to study and make predictions concerning currency or price movements in the forex market. He or she observes the patterns of the price like flags, double bottoms, and triangles on a chart and interprets the actions of the cost to find out the market conditions. As a result, he or she should have excellent analytical skills to evaluate the technical charts correctly. A trader that utilizes technical analysis has a short, medium, or long-term view of the trade he or she undertakes.

Technical analysis bases its operation on historical information about price movements since traders believe that history will repeat itself. They think that the price on the market will move in the same way as in the past if they find any similar historical patterns. A trader would be keen on a particular price level and build his or her trades on it if it provided a necessary price action in the past. Thus, he or she studies past movements of price and use that information to find out the current market conditions and possible price movements.

Technical analysis provides the visual representation of past movements of the price that inform a trader of the situation in the market. The price patterns and statistical trends in the analysis assist him or her to know the best time to enter or exit the market. Additionally, the technical signals also show him or her significant trading opportunities. Hence, technical analysis understanding can help a trader to make decisions that bring him or her gains. Simultaneously, it will also assist him or her to avoid trades or making unnecessary moves in the market that may result in considerable losses.

A trader uses various technical indicators to analyze the Forex Trading market, technically. Understanding how the indicators function can help him or her to comprehend the market conditions. Subsequently, he or she can then choose and apply the most appropriate trading strategy that will place him or her in the most profitable position in the market. The essential indicators that technical analysts employ in the forex market include:

1. Relative Strength Index Indicator (RSI)

The Relative Strength Index is an oscillator that provides a trader with signals to help him, or her sell high and buy low. It indicates to a trader the status of a currency, whereby it shows the overbought or oversold levels. The readings of an RSI indicator range from zero to 100, and they signal the speed and shift in price movements. The currency has overbought status when the value is above 70. Similarly, when the number on the oscillator is below 30, it indicates the oversold levels of that the currency.

Moreover, the RSI places the bullish and bearish price momentums against the price's graph and compares them. Bullish dynamics of the cost can cause overbought levels, while the bearish ones can produce oversold levels. As the forex market trends, a trader enters the trade in the trend's direction as the indicator recovers from the extremes. He or she finds the RSI going through a reversal from oversold levels or readings below 30 if there is an uptrend in the market. He or she then enters in the direction of that trend.

2. Slow Stochastic Indicator

The slow stochastic is an oscillator that helps a trader to identify profitable trade points in the forex market. It also assists him or her in determining the oversold and overbought levels in the trade. Its readings interpret the same as those of the RSI. It also uses the percentageK and the percentageD lines to indicate to the trader an entry point of a deal. The movements of these two lines on the oscillator will signal to the trader about a strong buying position that is in the direction of the price trend. A trader can take up such a place if the percentageK line crosses over the percentageD line through reading at the 20-level.

3. Moving Average Indicator

The moving average indicator helps a trader to determine trends, identify trade areas, and evaluate the forex markets. It assists him or her to establish the resistance and support levels as well as the patterns that indicate great buying or selling positions in the trade. A moving average indicator is also a lagging one because it also determines the current price direction, albeit with a lag. This delay stems from the signal utilizing historical data to establish the moving averages.

A trader can use the simple moving average (SMA) or the exponential moving average (EMA) to carry out the analysis. The SMA gives the simple mean of an asset in a given amount of time by adding all the closing prices and dividing the sum by the given number of days. If a trader uses a 20-day SMA, then he or she finds the total amount of the closing prices of the last 20 days and divides the total by 20.

An EMA provides the averages of the latest prices, unlike the SMA, which focuses on a long sequence of data points. A trader uses a particular formula to calculate the EMA, that is, Current EMA = [(Current closing price - (previous day EMA) × multiplier) +

previous day EMA]. The formula for the multiplier or smoothing constant in the above equation is 2/ (1+N), where N= the number of days.

A forex trader uses the momentum to determine the entry and exit points in the market. He or she enters the trade when the currency pair moves in the moving average's direction and exits when it runs in the opposite direction.

4. Moving Average Convergence Divergence Indicator (MACD)

This MACD indicator uses crossovers, divergences, and rapid rise and falls to show the link between moving averages of prices. In turn, it indicates the variations in momentum through a visual display, which helps a trader in recognizing a ranging or trending forex market. The calculation of the MACD involves the trader subtracting the 26-EMA period from the 12-EMA period, which provides him or her with the MACD line. A 9-day EMA of the MACD gives a trader the signal line in this indicator.

The trader can trade according to the movements of the MACD line concerning the signal line. He or she can buy when this line crosses beyond the signal line or sell when this line crosses beneath the signal line in the forex market. Moreover, the trader can determine a downward or upward bias of the currency pair by identifying the lines with regard to the zero lines.

He or she also can combine the MACD with a ranging or trending market to increase efficiency and minimize loss. The trader can place stops below the latest price extreme that is before the crossover. In doing so, he or she establishes a limit on the trade at the double the amount of his or her investment. The MACD provides the trader with suitable conditions when he or she uses crossovers of the MACD line in the trend's direction.

Fundamental Analysis

This methodology is the second type of analysis that a trader can use in the forex market. Unlike the technical analysis, this type concerns itself with the intrinsic value of an asset or currency. It evaluates the political, social, and economic factors that create a target price or establish value in the market. It uses information from features like interest rates, Gross Domestic Product (GDP), inflation, and others to analyze the trading conditions. A trader using fundamental analysis needs to have excellent analytical skills regarding statistical and economic data.

A fundamental trader in the forex market will assess a country's economic health by evaluating the trends of various data points and generally determine the strength and movements of the currency. He or she looks at various economic indicators and interprets them to find out the value of money. The essential economic signals that a trader can analyze the situation of the economy include:

1.   Inflation

Inflation is the increase in the quantity of money in circulation due to the growth of a country's economy. The more the money there is available, the more expensive the goods and services are in a country. When the economy of a state experiences too much inflation for an extended period, the associated currency becomes less valuable. The deprecation comes about because of there being too much supply of the money.

Conversely, the currency increases in value if an economy goes through deflation. Deflation takes place when there is little money in circulation. It leads to the country providing services and goods at lower prices. However, the value of the currency also drops when deflation carries on for a long time because there will be little money to support the economy. A country should balance the supply and demand aspects of its economy to ensure neither extreme devalues its currency.

2. Interest Rates

Interest rates are important indicators for fundamental analysis as they level the economy and can help a trader to discover trading opportunities. A common type of interest rate traders analyze is the nominal kind. The central banks create this nominal interest rate by referring to the principle that private banks pay to borrow currencies from them.

The central banks stimulate the individuals and private banks to borrow currency by lowering the interest rate as needed by the economy. It results in more valuable currency and improved performances in productivity, economics, and consumption. However, low-interest rates for extended periods can lead to there being too much money and form economic bubbles. Thus, the central bank balances the scale by cutting the prices of borrowing and providing less money for use by businesses, individuals, and banks.

3. Gross Domestic Product (GDP)

The gross domestic product provides the best indicator of a country's economic health by measuring all the services and goods that the state produces and supplies in a given period. Typically, a trader looks at the products and services in an economy in terms of supply and demand. However, the GDP focuses on the supply side of the analysis. The indicator assumes that the state made dependable and exact approximations based on a significant understanding of both supply and demand.

Hence, the increase in GDP should have a corresponding increase in gross domestic product demand. If the supply does not grow along with a rising GDP, it indicates that the economy is unhealthy. This indicator comes about because the economy in such a state shows that the goods and services provided are unaffordable.

Technical and fundamental analyses are critical in the evaluation and understanding of the forex market. The indicators provide visual information that helps a trader to comprehend and react quickly to the trade. The factors that influence a country's currency, such as economic indicators enable fundamental analysts to determine the cause for an increase of decrease in currency value. Therefore, learning elements that make up technical and fundamental analysis can assist a trader in achieving considerable success in Forex Trading.

Chapter 5: Psychology and Mindset of A Forex Trader

Human beings can be complicated and fascinating creatures. Many factors may influence how they think and behave in a given situation. However, at the base of every decision and reaction lie two essential features that ultimately determine a person's conduct. They are the attitude and personality of an individual. How a person sees things and the personality that he or she possesses will define his or her reaction to an event.

Similarly, the attitude and personality type of a forex trader will determine if he or she will succeed or fail in trading. These elements define his or her mindset as he or she enters and participates in the market. Thus, appropriately applying them can ensure a forex trader transacts successfully while simultaneously maintaining his or her psychological wellbeing. Here, we look at the mental mindset of a forex trader from two perspectives. The first angle is the attitude approach, and the second one is personality types.

Attitude Approach

The attitude of a forex trader determines how he or she views and interprets the market and its conditions. Having the right outlook is vital as it helps a trader to control his or her emotions and handle the vicissitudes of Forex Trading. Managing feelings and maintaining objectivity while trading will ensure success for a forex trader. The following are some of the attitudes that can help a trader to improve his or her mindset and achieve success in Forex Trading:

1.   Organization

An organized trader makes relevant preparations before and during a trade that enhances his or her chances of success. A person should have an organization in all the steps involved in the trading, including decisions before entering a forex trade:

- **Create a Trading Plan** – A trading plan provides a trader with a sequence of what is taking place in the market and some expectations. It helps him or her to keep track of the market conditions in a systematic way that facilitates effective decision-making.

- **Think Before Entering a Trade** – A trader should carry out extensive research regarding the trade and weigh all possible options before starting. He or she should be as objective and logical as possible when deciding to enter the market.

- **Maintain a Record of the Trades** – A trading journal is essential in Forex Trading as it provides the trader with relevant feedback concerning his or her situation on the market.

2.   Confidence

Having confidence in the market is booster as it helps a trader to avoid making rash decisions or switching back and forth.

- **Have Full Confidence in the Decisions** – Having belief and full confidence in the decision a trader makes is vital as it signifies that he or she does not fear the trade. He or she analyzed everything in detail and logically came to that particular decision. Hence, he or she does not worry, even if he or she does lose in the end.

- **Following the Map of Price Action** – A trader should trust the information that price action provides. It indicates the market conditions and offers a useful guideline that can help a trader to make decisions without the influence of emotions.

- **Avoid Gambling** – A confident attitude helps a trader to avoid gambling in the market because he or she does not panic. Instead, he or she takes time to evaluate the situation before making a move.

3.   Patience

Patience is a virtue that also applies to a forex trader. Keeping calm despite the profits and losses in the markets can help a trader to avoid the dangers of reacting emotionally in the markets.

- **Value Quality Over Quantity** – Being patient enables a trader to make profits consistently for an extended period. He or she will receive small benefits but will last for a much longer time, rather than rushing for huge gains and losing trade quickly.

- **Use the Daily Charts to Learn** – Learning using the daily charts enable a trader to develop an outlook of looking at the bigger picture of the market. It will also allow him or her to practice some trading strategies and make appropriate corrections before entering the forex market.

4.   Realistic Expectation

Understanding the trade and having realistic expectations will go a long way into helping a trader to succeed in Forex Trading. It helps him or her to make the right plans, use appropriate strategies and decisions in the market. It also helps to keep his or her emotions in check.

- **Understand the Independence of Each Trade** – Regardless of previous experiences, a trader must understand and identify each trade as a different transaction. It helps the trader know that the next trade's success or failure is absolute.

- **Trade Using Disposable Capital** – A trader should trade using only disposable capital. He or she should risk the money that he or she does not need; otherwise, he or she should not enter the trade.

- **Avoid Sleepless Nights** – A trader should not continue with a trade that he or she doubts. He or she should drop it if he or she loses sleep due to worrying about the risks involving his or her investment.

- **Do Not Take Trades Personally** – A trader should not have an emotional attachment to the trade. Doing so assists him or her to avoid taking the trades personally and view the forex market as a fluctuating trading environment.

5.   Learning from Each Experience

Lastly, a person needs to take every experience from the market as a learning lesson. He or she needs to take into account the aspects and decisions that led to the success of failure of a particular transaction. This lesson is even more important in Forex Trading because recognizing the errors made can enable a trader to convert a loss into a profit. He or she looks at the mistakes involved, analyzes every decision, and the subsequent reactions in the market.

The failed trades will provide a trader with relevant information such as clues for what the mistake is and the reasons for the loss. Failures tend to offer a trader relevant information that can enable a forex trader to succeed in the future by avoiding repeating mistakes.

Personality Types of Traders

A person can also look at the psychological mindset of a forex trader from the perspective of the personality. Each individual has his or her personality trait that defines who he or she is. Every personality type consists of different strengths and weaknesses. Forex Trading, as is with other similar transactions, can produce a considerable profit at the moment but cause significant losses at another.

A trader experiences various emotion when it comes to dealing with money matters. He or she invests and trades his or her money to receive profits. He or she also wants to minimize risks and avoid losses as much as possible. Hence, whenever the trader experiences significant gains or losses, he or she goes through strong emotions that bring out his or her personality. The type of character that a trader has is essential because it determines how he or she will behave in the trading market. The trader's personality will define how he or she thinks, the decisions he or she makes, and the subsequent actions.

Therefore, a person needs to understand the various types of personality that a trader can possess. This knowledge will help him or her to comprehend why some traders make individual decisions in particular periods. Additionally, it will enable the individual to study his or her behavior and identify the personality kind that describes him or her. As a result, the person can recognize his or her strengths and weaknesses. It will enable him or her to know the area to improve.

Learning and understanding these types of personalities can help a person to determine the ones that suit Forex Trading the best. He or she will be able to identify and adopt the personality kind that brings about consistent gains in the trading processes. A beginner in Forex Trading can have a chance to prepare himself or herself better before entering the trade. An experienced trader can get more knowledge that will assist him or her to make appropriate enhancements that eventually lead to improved profits and overall success. The following are some of the essential types of personalities and the characteristics that describe them.

1. The Detailed Type

As the name suggests, a detailed trader pays attention to the details of the trade. He or she takes his or her time to look carefully before leaping into a transaction. The trader uses rationality to evaluate the entire situation and everything relating to the market before trading. He or she logically and systematically carry out relevant researches, take detailed notes, and combine all the information received to inform his or her decision.

Furthermore, the trader with this personality also writes trading notes regarding his or her situation in the market. He or she inputs the reasons for writing the points that he or she has and utilizes them to determine the next moves in the market. The attention to detail helps a trader to make decisions that have minimal risks. Conversely, he or she can waste time analyzing before entering a market and end up losing on potentially profitable trades.

2. The Innovative Type

A trader with an innovative personality is instinctive and thinks on his or her feet. He or she uses his or her intuitive skills to read people and events, think and make judgments when trading. Trading involves making the right moves at the correct time to ensure one does not incur losses and, instead, receive profits. An innovative trader carefully analyzes the information available and makes appropriate decisions to form or improve a trade. He or she uses creativity to assess and interpret the information at hand.

Additionally, the creative thinking that a trader with this personality possesses enables him or her to reach relevant conclusions quickly. He or she observes and interprets the significant meanings from large amounts of feedback and information. The trader then swiftly takes immediate action that helps to take advantage or solve issues arising from the market conditions. The innovative traders are keen, quick thinkers, and decisive. This personality provides them with features that can make good leaders.

3. The Playful Type

A trader possessing a playful personality kind has a fun-loving nature. He or she enters and carries out a trade with a playful attitude. This trader is optimistic, in that, he or she sees the bright side of things. He or she views the business as one that will succeed, even if a current transaction is causing losses. He or she also has a lot of positivity that makes him or her have a playful approach to the trade.

Moreover, a trader with this personality involves a certain level of social interaction as he or she trades. He or she communicates and includes other people in his or her thoughts regarding a trade. He or she may even take some advice from other traders about a particular problem. Nevertheless, the weakness of a playful trader type is that he or she is emotional due to his or her positive and optimistic characteristics. Sometimes he or she lets his or her sentiments cloud his or her rationality in the thought and decision-making processes.

4. The Spontaneous Type

A trader with a spontaneous personality does not spend time evaluating and making detailed trading strategies in a trade. He or she has a hard time concentrating on such details. Instead, he or she thinks about a situation as it occurs in the market and makes a decision quickly. The lack of concrete strategies and analysis may expose him or her to avoidable risks that he or she may not expect.

5. The Values-Driven Type

A trader with a values-driven personality is independent in his or her approach to the market. He or she does not follow the crowd and, instead, weighs up the situation, thinks carefully, and makes the relevant trading decisions. Additionally, a value-driven trader concerns himself or herself with certain aspects regarding the trade. He or she emphasizes factors such as relationships, ideas, and the substantial returns of a transaction. Independence enables this trader to look at the bigger picture of the market and make reliable decisions.

However, his or her weakness lies in the emotions that he or she experiences while trading. The trader puts significance that is more considerable on his or her values, which can lead to missed opportunities. Emotions can also make him or her less logical when analyzing the markets.

6. The Administrative Type

An administrative trader adapts to changes and makes effective decisions accordingly. He or she is realistic and practical about the trades and makes sensible moves in the market. He or she can lead other traders or delegate when necessary.

7. The Accurate Type

An accurate trader is attentive to details. He or she applies a detailed evaluation of the situation and notes down every detail concerning the trade. He or she uses a Forex Trading journal to record every assessment and market condition. He or she refers to these details to help him or her to analyze or solve a particular problem.

8. The Independent Type

A trader with an independent personality type does not follow other people's decisions. The trading market is always moving, and it can easily lead to traders making judgments according to the crowd. Emotions can cause someone to allow the decisions and actions of others to determine his or her moves in the market. However, the independent trader thinks for himself or herself.

This trader observes the situation, studies it, and even tries to look at it from different points of view. Once he or she assesses the state of the market, he or she makes the most suitable decision for his or her trades. An independent trader uses creativity and innovatively to come up with strategies and solutions to any issues that arise in his or her transactions. Consequently, the trader's independence causes him or her to be a weak team player because he or she does not have strong social skills.

9. The Facilitative Type

A trader with a facilitative personality trades in a precise and systematic manner. He or she regards trading as a serious business and uses a sober attitude when dealing in the market. He or she meaningfully think about the appropriate moves to make in the transaction and makes the final choices in an organized manner. He or she looks at not only his or her trades but also the entire market. It forms a bigger picture that informs his or her judgments.

Besides, a facilitative trader likes to engage with other traders in the market. Unlike the independent type, this trader enjoys trading in a social setting where he or she gets to work while sharing ideas with others. As a result, the facilitative trader can succeed when cooperating with others, such as in trading partnerships or teams.

10.   The Socially Responsible Type

A trader with a socially responsible personality places great importance on the values he or she holds dear. Accordingly, he or she makes strategies and decisions that are in line with these values. He or she also only takes up new chances or makes moves in the market that are in consonance with his or her social ideologies. Aside from respecting and upholding the values of interest, the trader also takes delight in social life. Thus, he or she enjoys a social life while being responsible for maintaining significant social ideology.

11. The Artistic Type

A trader with an artistic personality type uses creativity and intuition while trading. He or she employs his or her artistry and uses creative and original thinking processes to make relevant moves in the market. An artistic trader is more creative and intuitive when compared to other traders in the business.

Likewise, he or she possesses flexibility in the personality that allows him or her to change and adapt to different conditions in trading. Despite this, he or she must take care not to let his or her emotions cloud his or her judgment. He or she should be wary of too much emotional connection with the trades.

12. The Supportive Type

A supportive trader owns portions of the qualities that make up complete and successful traders. The characteristics that he or she possesses enable him or her to provide support to others in the trading world. A trader with this type of personality is conscious, with a lot of insight into the factors associated with the market. He or she also approaches transactions with a somber attitude that helps him or her to make sound decisions in the trade. These qualities attract other traders; in that, they make the supportive trader dependable.

13.   The Adventurous Type

A trader with an adventurous personality experiences great success while trading. The success comes from the fact that he or she utilizes factual data to make any judgments regarding the market. He or she uses data to evaluate the situation of the trade rationally before making appropriate decisions. As a result, he or she applies a systematic thought process and makes the most sensible choices that lead to success. Furthermore, an adventurous trader tends to take more risks in the market.

The more the risk there is in a trade, the higher the returns a trader will receive. Thus, he or she utilizes his or her flexible mind to assess a market critically and decide whether he is open to a particular trade. Consequently, the adventurous trader is decisive in trading as he or she uses facts, logic, and analysis to make productive and profitable decisions. Nonetheless, he or she must take care not to push his or her sense of adventure too far. The trader should be mindful of taking too many risks as the strategy may backfire and lead to considerable losses.

Ultimately, the main factors that significantly determine and influence the psychological mindset of a forex trader are emotions and the types of personality. The hope of receiving profits and the fear of losing money can drive a person to make decisions that can make trading success or complete failure. An individual need to understand the characteristics, personality, and attitude that an individual has. Understanding these elements of a person can enable a trader to know how to improve his or her approach to Forex Trading. He or she can also learn the dos and don'ts when dealing with the pressures of Forex Trading. In all, the knowledge from such comprehension will help a trader to enhance his or her mindset to ensure Forex Trading success.

Chapter 6: Forex Strategies and Strategies for Beginners

Forex Trading strategy is what forex traders do to buy or sell financial instruments at a given time to generate profits. Forex Trading strategies are nowadays done, either manually or automatically. A trader is using manual strategies when he or she interprets the trading signals and as a result, decides to buy or sell. The automated method is where a trader comes up with an algorithm that studies the trading signals and executes trades on its own.

Before choosing a Forex Trading strategy, it is important to identify which of these four trading styles fits your personality:

1. Day Trading

Day trading is a short-term trading style designed to buy and sell financial securities within the same trading day. That is closing all positions by the end of the trading day. In Day Trading, you can hold your trades for minutes or even hours. Day traders deal with financial instruments like options, stock, currencies, and contracts for difference. Many day traders are investment firms and banks. Day traders use technical analysis to make trading decisions.

Pros

- Day traders are not affected by unmanageable risks and negative price gaps because all positions are closed by the end of the trading day.
- There are a substantial number of trading opportunities
- Traders can be extremely profitable due to the rapid returns

Cons

- Traders can be extremely unprofitable due to the rapid returns
- You don't have to be concerned with the economy or long-term trends
- Huge opportunity cost
- Day traders have to exit a losing position very quickly, to prevent a greater loss.

2. Swing Trading

Swing trading is where a trader holds an asset between one and several days in an attempt to capture gains in the financial market. This type of traders doesn't monitor the screens all day, and they do it a few hours a day. Swing traders usually rely on technical analysis to look for trading opportunities. Swing trading position is held longer than day trading position but shorter than buy and hold investments. They have larger profit targets than day traders.

Pros

- Swing traders can rely solely on technical analysis, which simplifies the process
- Requires less time to trade compared to day-trading

Cons

- Swing traders are exposed to overnight and weekend risks
- Generally, swing trading risks are as a result of market speculation
- It is difficult to know when to enter and exit a trade when swing trading

3. Scalping Trading

Scalping is the fastest trading style where traders hold positions for a very short time frame. Traders here gain profits due to small price changes. The scalpers hold a position for a short period to gain profits. Traders with large amounts of capital or bid-offers spread narrowly prefer scalping. Scalping follows four principles:

- Small moves are more frequent - even when the market is quiet, scalpers can make hundreds or thousands of trades
- Small moves are easier to obtain - small moves happen all the time compared to large ones
- Less risky than larger moves - scalpers only hold positions for short periods therefore because they have less exposure the risk is also lower
- Spreads can be both bonuses and costs. Spread is the numerical difference between the bid and ask prices. Various parties and different strategies view spread as either trading bonuses or costs.

Pros

- Positions can be liquidated quickly, usually within minutes or seconds
- Very profitable when used as a primary strategy
- It's a low-risk strategy
- Scalpers are not exposed to overnight risks

Cons

- Requires an exit strategy especially during large losses
- Not the best strategy for beginners; it involves quick decision-making abilities.

4. Position Trading

Position trading involves holding a position open for a long period expecting it to appreciate. Traders here can hold positions for weeks, months, or even years. Position traders are not concerned with short-term fluctuations; they are keener on long-term views that affect their positions. Position trading is not done actively. Most traders place an average of 10 trades a year.

This strategy seeks to capture full gains of long-term trading, which would result in an appreciation of their investment capital. Position traders use fundamental analysis, technical analysis, or a combination of both to make trading decisions. To succeed position, traders need plans in place to control risk as well as identify the entry and exit levels.

Pros

- Traders have a longer period to reap fruits.
- Trader's time is not on demand. Once the trade has been initiated, all they can do is wait for the desired outcome

Cons

- Traders may fall victim to opportunity costs because capital is usually tied up for longer periods.
- Position traders tend to ignore minor fluctuations, which can turn to trend reversals, a change in the price direction of a position.

Forex Trading Strategies

There are several types of forex strategies; however, it is important to choose the right one based preferred trading style to trade successfully. Some strategies work on short-term trades as well as long-term trades. The type of Forex strategies you choose depends on a few factors like:

- Entry points - traders need to determine the appropriate time to enter the market
- Exit point-trader need to develop rules on when to exit the market as well as how to get out of a losing position
- Time availability

If you have a full-time job, then you cannot use day trading or scalping styles

- Personal choices

People who prefer lower winning rates but larger gains should go for position trading while those who prefer higher winning rate but smaller gains can choose the swing trading

Common Forex Trading strategies include:

1. Range trading strategy

Range trading is one of the many viable trading strategies. This strategy is where a trader identifies the support and resistance levels and buys at the support level and sells at the resistance level. This strategy works when there is a lack of market direction or the absence of a trend. Range trading strategies can be broken down into three steps:

- **Finding the Range**

Finding the range uses the support and resistance zones. The support zone is the buying price of the security while the resistance zone price is the selling price of a security. A breakout happens in the event that the price goes beyond the trading range, whereas a breakdown occurs in the event that the price goes below the trading range.

- **Time Your Entry**

Traders use a variety of indicators like price action and volume to enter and exit the trading range. They can also use oscillators like CCI, RSI, and stochastics to time their entry. The oscillators track prices using mathematical calculations. Then the traders wait for the prices to reach the support or resistance zones. They often strike when the momentum turns price in the opposing direction.

- **Managing Risk**

The last step is risk management. When the level of support or resistance breaks, traders will want to exit any range-based positions. They can either use a stop loss above the previous high or invert the process with a stop below the current low.

Pros

- There are ranges that can last even for years producing multiple winning trades.

Cons

- Long-lasting ranges are not easy to come by, and when they do, every range trader wants to use it.
- Not all ranges are worth trading

2. Trend Trading Strategy

Another popular and common Forex Trading strategy is the trend trading strategy. This strategy attempts to make profits by analyzing trends. The process involves identifying an upward or downward trend in a currency price movement and choosing trade entry and exit points based on the currency price within the trend.

Trend traders use these four common indicators to evaluate trends; moving averages, relative strength index (RSI), On-Balance-Volume (OBV), and Moving Average Convergence Divergence (MACD). These indicators provide trend trade signals, warn of reversals, and simplify price information. A trader can combine several indicators to trade.

Pros

- Offers a better risk to reward
- Can be used across any markets

Cons

- Learning to trade on indicators can be challenging.

3. Pairs Trade

This is a neutral trading strategy, which allows pair traders to gain profits in any market conditions. This strategy uses two key strategies:

- Convergence trading - this strategy focuses on two historically correlated securities, where the trader buys one asset forward and sells a similar asset forward for a higher price anticipating that prices will become equal. Profits are made when the underperforming position gains value, and the outperforming position's price deflates

- Statistical trading - this is a short-term strategy that uses the mean reversion models involving broadly diversified Security Portfolios. This strategy uses data mining and statistical methods.

Pros

- If pair trades go as expected investors can make profits

Cons

- This strategy relies on a high statistical correlation between two securities, which can be a challenge.

- Pairs trade relies a lot on historical trends, which do not depict future trends accurately.

4. Price Action Trading

This Forex Trading strategy involves analyzing the historical prices of securities to come up with a trading strategy. Price action trading can be used in short, medium, and long periods. The most commonly used price action indicator is the price bar, which shows detailed information like high and low-price levels during a specific period. However, most traders use more than one strategy to recognize trading patterns, stop-losses, and entry, and exit levels. Technical analysis tools also help price action traders make decisions.

Pros

- No two traders will interpret certain price action the same way

Cons

- Past price history cannot predict future prices accurately

5. Carry Trade Strategy

Carry trade strategy involves borrowing a low-interest currency to buy a currency that has a high rate; the goal is to make a profit with the interest rate difference. For example, one can buy currency pairs like the Japanese yen (low interest) and the Australian dollar (high interest) because the interest rate spreads are very high. Initially, carry trade was used as a one-way trade that moved upwards without reversals, but carry traders soon discovered that everything went downhill once the trade collapsed.

With the carry trade strategy:

1. You need to first identify which currencies offer high rates and which ones have low rates.

2. Then match two currencies with a high-interest differential

3. Check whether the pair has been in an upward tendency favoring the higher-interest rate currency

Pros

- The strategy works in a low volatility environment.
- Suitable for a long-term strategy
- **Cons**
- Currency rates can change anytime
- Ricky because they are highly leveraged
- Used by many traders therefore overcrowded

6. Momentum Trading

This strategy involves buying and selling assets according to the strength of recent price trends. The basis for this strategy is that an asset price that is moving strongly in a given direction will continue to move in the same direction until the trend loses strength. When assets reach a higher price, they tend to attract many investors and traders who push the market price even higher. This continues until large pools of sellers enter the market and force the asset price down.Momentum traders identify how strong trends are in a given direction. They open positions to take advantage of the expected price change and close positions when the prices go down.

There are two kinds of momentum:

- Relative momentum - different securities within the same class are compared against each other, and then traders and investors buy strong performing ones and sell the weak ones.

- Absolute momentum - an asset's price is compared against its previous performance.

Pros

- Traders can capitalize on volatile market trends
- Traders can gain high profit over a short period
- This strategy can take advantage of changes in stock prices caused by emotional investors.

Cons

- A momentum investor is always at a risk of timing a buy incorrectly.
- This strategy works best in a bull market; therefore, it is market sensitive
- This strategy is time-intensive; investors need to keep monitoring the market daily.
- Prices can shift in a different direction anytime

7. Pivot Points

This strategy determines resistance and support levels using the average of the previous trading sessions, which predict the next prices. They take the average of the high, low, and closing prices. A pivot point is a price level used to indicate market movements. Bullish sentiment occurs when one trades above the pivot point while bearish sentiment occurs when one trades below the pivot point.

Pros

- Traders can use the levels to plan out their trading in advance because prices remain the same throughout the day
- Works well with other strategies

Cons

- Some traders do not find pivot points useful
- There is no guarantee that price will stop or reverse at the levels created on the chart

8. Fundamental Analysis

This strategy involves analyzing the economic, social, and political forces that may affect the supply and demand of an asset. Usually, people use supply and demand to gauge which direction the price is headed to. The Fundamental analysis strategy then analyzes any factors that may affect supply and demand. By assessing these factors, traders can determine markets with a good economy and those with a bad one.

Forex Strategies for Beginners

When starting on Forex Trading, it important to keep things simple. As a beginner, avoid thinking about money too much and focus on one or two strategies at a time. The following three strategies are easy to understand and perfect for beginners.

1. Inside Bar Trading Strategy

This highly effective strategy is a two-bar price action strategy with an inside bar and a prior/mother bar. The inside bar is usually smaller and within the high and low range of the prior bar. There are many variations of the inside bar, but what remains constant is that the prior bar always fully engulfs the inside bar. Although very profitable, the inside bar setup does not occur often.

There are two main ways you can trade using inside bars:

- As a continuation move - This is the easiest way to trade inside bars. The inside bars are traded in trending markets following the direction of the trend.

- As a reversal pattern - the inside bars are traded counter-trend

When using this strategy, it is important to look for these characteristics when evaluating the pattern:

- Time frame matters - avoid any time frame less than the daily.
- Focus on the breakout - best inside bar trades happen after a break of consolidation where the preceding trend is set to resume.
- The trend Is your friend - trading with the trend is the only way to trade an inside bar
- A favorable risk to reward ratio is needed when trading an inside bar
- The size of the inside bar in comparison to the prior bar is extremely important

2. Pin Bar Trading Strategy

This strategy is highly recommended for beginners because it is easy to learn due to a better visual representation of price action on a chart. It is one of the easiest strategies to trade. Pin bars show a reversal in the market and, therefore, can be useful in predicting the direction of the price. Pin bars consist of one price bar, known as a candlestick price bar, which represents a sharp reversal and rejection of price. Candlestick charts are the clearest at showing price action.

There are various ways traders trading with pin bars can enter the market:

- At the current market price
- Using an on-stop entry

- At limit entry, which is at the 50% retrace of the pin bar

To improve your odds when using the pin bar strategy:

- Trade with the trend
- Wait for a break of structure
- Trade from an area of value

Some of the mistakes pin bar traders should avoid include the following:

- Assuming the market will reverse because of a pin bar
- Focus too much on the pin bars and miss out on other trading opportunities
- All pin bars are not the same and should not be treated as such

3. Forex Breakout Strategy

A breakout strategy is where investors find stocks that have built strong support or resistance level, wait for a breakout, and enter the market when momentum is in their favor. This strategy is important because it can offer expansions in volatility, major price moves, and limited risk. A breakout occurs when the price moves beyond the support or resistance level. The breakout strategy is good for beginners because they can catch every trend in the market. Breakouts occur in all types of market environments.

Traders establish a bullish position when prices are set to close above a resistance level and a bearish position when prices close below a support level. Sometimes traders can be caught on a false breakout, and the only way to determine if it is a false breakout is to wait for confirmation. False breakout prices usually go beyond the support and resistance level; however, they return to a prior trading range by the end of the day.

Good investors plan how they will exit the markets before establishing a position. With breakouts, there are two exit plans:

- Where to exit with profit-traders can assess the stock recent behaviors to determine reasonable objectives. When traders meet their goals, they can exit the position. They can either raise a stop-loss to lock in profits or exit a portion of the position to let the rest run

- Where to exit with a loss - breakout trading show traders clearly when a trade has failed, and therefore they can determine where to set stop-loss order.

Traders can use the old support or resistance level to close a losing trade

Pros

- You can catch every trend in the market
- ·Prices can quickly move in your favor

Cons

- Traders can get caught in a false breakout
- It can be difficult to enter a trade

Tips for trading breakouts:

- Never sell on breakdown or buy on breakout both carry extreme risks
- Trade with the trend
- Wait for higher volume to confirm a breakout
- Take advantage of volatility cycles
- Enter on the retest of support or resistance
- Have a predetermined exit plan

Note

Beginners are more likely to be successful in trade than their experienced counterparts are because they have not yet cultivated any bad habits. Experienced traders have to break bad habits and put aside any emotions built over the years.

Chapter 7: Forex Trading Signals

How can a forex trader find out which Forex pair and time frame is best to buy or sell? For starters, the forex trader can move from one chart to another to identify the forex market trend. However, in view of the fact that markets change from time to time, switching through charts can be a tedious exercise. Additionally, some patterns may be erratic and unpredictable, and therefore fail to make a profit.

Nevertheless, if a forex trader could find a way to examine all the currency pairs swiftly and time frames to find the best trend, he or she can expect a dramatic increase in profitability in any method he or she trades. Forex Trading signals can help forex traders make such critical decisions about profiting from their investments.

What Are Forex Trading Signals?

Put simply, Forex Trading signals are guidelines and recommendations that help inexperienced forex traders to open Forex Trading positions. The signals are a type of system that forex traders use to make crucial decisions about their trade. In that regard, Forex Trading signals provide details about how to open a new Forex Trade.

Examples of such details include details about which currency pair to trade, when to open the trade (open date), whether to buy or sell (position), and information on the opening price. In addition, they provide details on the stop-loss level to set if the forex market starts to experience loses, and the target profit level, that is, the point at which the trade should close so that forex traders can secure their profits.

Accurate and timely signals help forex traders to have success in their trade, whereas wrong signals reduce the opportunity for forex traders to earn and to make profits from their investments.

Forex Trading signals send email alerts that show trading arrangements for the next 24-hours. Various Forex Trading signals providers give free trial services that allow currency traders to become familiar with signal illustrations to calculate the values of the currencies. In that way, currency traders are able to evaluate the quality and the reliability of the Forex Trading signals before traders can pay subscription money.

When looking through Forex signals services, the forex trader must ensure that the Forex Trading signal provider offers the type of signals the forex trader needs.

Types of Forex Trading Signals and How They Work

Each signal is different from the other, and every forex trader needs to have a basic idea of the operation of the two types of Forex Trading signals. A forex trader can choose the type of signal to use, depending on his or her needs and depending on the signal's function.

Manual Forex Trading Signals

Manual forex signals require human traders to analyze the market before Forex signal providers distribute the signals. The human traders comprise of a team of financial analysts and experienced forex traders who carry out Forex market analysis and open the trading signals.

When the traders receive signals, they log into their Forex account and key in the trades. That means that the trader will need to be available at all times to key in the trades.

What are the benefits of Manual Forex Trading Signals?

Higher Profit Targets: The profit targets in manual trading signals are typically more significant than in the automated trading signals unless the signal provider uses a scalping tactic. Profit targets help forex traders to reduce risk by establishing a target price when the forex trader wants to take profits on a trade.

Consequently, manual signals that large financial institutions offer their clients target hundreds of pips when the high-frequency signals target fractions of a pip. A pip is short for 'point in percentage,' and it is a significantly small measure of variation in a currency pair in the Forex market.

For example, if a currency sells at 3.6997, and buys at 3.6999, then the pip is 2.

Useful Trading Tools: Manual trading signals are indicators that highlight excellent trading prospects. A forex trader can conduct his or her own forex market analysis, come up with his or her own plan and strategy, and use the manual signals to crosscheck his or her evaluation.

The use of manual signals also enables the forex trader to sort out risk levels depending on the conditions of the forex market. A forex trader is in charge of all the trading functions. Therefore, when the forex market is volatile, the forex trader can reduce the number of currency units that he or she will buy, and increase the size once the market stabilizes.

Profitable Risk-Reward Ratios: Risk – reward ratios measure how much a forex trader's potential reward is, for every amount of money that he or she risks. For example, if a forex trader has a risk-reward ratio of 1:5, it means that the forex trader is risking $1 to make $5 theoretically. It is, however, not definite that the trader will earn $5.

Consequently, manual signals often provide risk-reward ratios of 1:1 or better, compared to the automated signals, which give a minimum of 1:2 risk-reward ratio. Even with a risk-reward ratio of 1:0.5, a forex trader stands to gain $0.5 for every dollar he or she trades over the long term.

Trading News Releases: Trading news is an approach to buy or sell equities, currencies, and other financial instruments in the forex markets. Manual forex traders issue out outcomes of the news releases in ways that offer significant winning potential.

Manual forex traders or financial analysts examine news reports and identify the causes that will cause the forex market to move in a specific direction. Therefore, the forex signal providers issue out manual signals from the financial analysts, which predict what numbers, will be released.

With such expectation, forex investors start trading before the release of the actual numbers. That is unlike using trading robots, which are not always able to trade the outcomes of the news releases.

Flexibility: Manual Forex Trading signals have the capacity to adjust to market changes and fluctuations. Forex investors make profits by buying or selling as many currencies as they can.

Consequently, when a forex investor receives a manual trading signal for a trade, which appears to be heading in a profitable direction, the forex signal provider may extend that take profit level and increase the profit productively. Thus, manual Forex Trading signals provide forex investors with suck kind of flexibility in the forex market.

Human Experience: One of the most positive aspects of manual Forex Trading signals is human intelligence and expertise, which cannot compare to that of computers. Many skilled forex traders have a good feel of the forex market and can, therefore, tell the best time for buying or selling to gain profitable trades. Robots do not often perceive such upward or downward trends.

Because crowd psychology drives the forex market, human reasoning ingrains manual trading signals. As a result, the manual signals can manipulate the market trends for maximum profitability.

What are the shortcomings of Manual Forex Trading Signals?

Manual trading signals are suitable for extending profit targets, but the process of issuing out signals can be time-consuming. Even though manual signal providers may not need to conduct all the forex market analysis, they still have to open the Forex Trading platform and carry on with the trading business.

Additionally, manual signal providers are not able to follow the manual signals distributed during nighttime or work hours. In addition, manual trading signal providers do not have extensive coverage of a variety of other currency pairs. That is because many signal providers focus their attention on significant currency pairs, thus leaving out other financial instruments that include cryptocurrencies, stock indices, and commodities.

Automated Forex Trading Signals

Automated Forex signals have robotic programs, which analyze the market before the forex signal providers issue out the signals.

Due to the impracticality of trading forex on a part-time basis, many forex investors, brokers, and independent financial institutions have created trading systems that distribute forex signals that tell the user when to trade.

With automated Forex Trading, buying or selling can be as simple as pushing a button or making a telephone call to the signal provider.

What are the benefits of Automated Forex Trading Signals?

It Does Not Involve Any Paperwork: Signal providers do not go through any complex processes involving paperwork, in order for them to get started on distribution signals.

It Saves Time: A person does not have to remain transfixed on their computer monitors or screens all day long to buy or sell. The automated trading robot takes care of all the tasks 24-hours a day.

Similarly, one does not have to spend time coming up with his or her own trading plan. Instead, a person can choose to follow a forex trader who has a similar Forex Trading strategy and risk profile as his or her own. In that way, the person will have more time to set trades and to keep an eye on different forex markets.

In addition, forex traders and signal providers do not have to worry about missing trades because automated trading performs trades much faster than any human being.

Passive Trading: Automated Forex Trading signals are not subject to any human emotions, and therefore, are a clear-cut set of rules to follow.

Easily Accessible to Beginners: Precise automated forex signals help beginner forex traders to learn how experienced traders buy or sell. Beginners can achieve this by replicating the trades of the more experienced traders who have shared their successful strategies.

Similarly, beginners do not need to have minimum balances in their Forex Trading accounts to begin trading. Furthermore, automated signals can boost the confidence of beginner traders concerning the forex market. Beginner traders can relate their analysis to that of their signal's provider and thereby learn more about Forex Trading while accumulating profits.

Independent Control of Trading Account: Only the forex traders and signal providers can access their accounts. What's more, traders sign in the account in their name, and they do not have to give a power of attorney to any other person.

Back-Testing Trading Strategies: Trading robots have the ability to use historical data to evaluate the viability of a trading strategy and thus finding out how the plan will play out in the forex market.

Forex traders can fine-tune such strategies to yield outcomes that are more positive. When the trading robot performs the back-testing, signal providers can confidently open their trade because the providers will have a better idea of how the trading robots will perform in the future.

What are the disadvantages of Automated Forex Trading Signals?

Automated Forex Trading signals are not flexible. There are times when a forex investor may need to manipulate a trade or to forego a deal when the market goes in the opposite direction.

For example, when news breaks out about a hurricane hitting the investor's country, the investor will know that the trading platform will not remain stable. As a result, the investor may end up making losses following the effects the hurricane will have on assets sold on the trading platform.

Additionally, an automated Forex Trading account can breakdown potentially creating significant issues. A computerized trading account can stop endorsing trades, thus leaving trades to linger or cause the system to crash entirely. Alternatively, the automated account can have a technical error or a virus in the software where forex traders can lose all the money in their accounts at once.

How to Choose the Best Trading Signals

How can one know how to choose the best trading signals? Below are the factors a person should consider in making that decision.

The Regularity of Trading Signals: In the search for the best trading signals in the forex market, a trader should look for signal providers who issue favorable trading signals and alerts recurrently. That is because signals will not take too long to appear even if a person misses one or two signals. In that way, a trader can become consistent with his or her trading.

Variety of Financial Instruments: Signal providers who offer signals on diverse financial tools make it possible for a forex trader to choose investments from a wide range of options. Outstanding trading signals on commodities, currency pairs, stock indices, and cryptocurrencies give forex traders access to various financial instruments across different asset classifications.

Negligible Drawdowns: Choose signal providers who have minimal and negligible consecutive losing trades, but have solid equity growth curves. That will help in producing excellent performance in terms of investment profitability.

Constant Profits: It is essential to identify trading signals with excellent and consistent trading outcomes. A forex trader can accomplish this by choosing signal providers who are experts at analyzing the forex market and are therefore able to adapt to the continually changing market conditions.

Experienced signal providers demonstrate a focused effort in providing regular forex signals of the highest quality.

Therefore, how can a person know how to choose the best Forex Trading signal providers?

Credible Profitability History: Is there evidence of unrealistic profits? A forex trader should smell a rat when a signal provider issues out signals with five or more pips profit from a trade. That level of profit would be unrealistic and not trustworthy.

Consequently, a forex trader should search for signal providers who have authenticated track records. The best option would be to verify the track records through third-party online verification facilities.

The Timing of the Signal: It is wise for a forex trader to outline the schedule of the signals. That is because the trader may not have a lot of time to spend in front of his or her computer waiting for the signal provider to issue out a signal.

In order not to miss out on signals, a forex trader should check the signal provider's time zone and master the times during which the signal provider sends out signals. That is an important consideration to think about before signing up for a Forex Trading signal service.

Trial periods can help a forex trader to know the times the signal providers distribute signals.

Free Trial Period: It would be wise for a person to choose a signal provider who gives a free trial period. That will prevent the person from getting into the market without knowing how the signals work and possibly risking all of his or her investment.

Knowing whether a signal provider is right or not helps a person to develop trust with the provider. Trial periods provide opportunities for a person to test the signals and to confirm whether the set-up of the signals conforms to his or her trading style.

Random Signals: Some Forex Trading signal providers distribute random signals that seem to have no apparent strategy. Robots could generate such signals, which may lack thorough analysis.

Consequently, a forex trader should evaluate the trading positions of the signals – are they long-term or short-term? In addition, the trader should check to see whether the signals are founded on technical analysis, or fundamental analysis, or a mix of both.

Therefore, a person should evaluate signals to know whether they will be suitable for his or her trading style.

Details About the Signal Performance: Are the details short and simple? Aspects such as entry point, stop loss, and take profits should be easily understandable so that a forex trader can visualize all the factors to decide whether a signal is lucrative and appropriate.

The best Forex Trading signals, therefore, take into account definitions and forex market assessments that associate with the Forex Trading signals. Forex traders may not feel confident to use signals that do not explain why a forex trader should open a particular trade.

Are the Signals Easy to Follow? Forex Trading signals that are easy to follow are those that are in a well-organized format. The structure will, therefore, have definite entry and exit prices and stop loss figures. These will help in financial management and the steady growth of a forex trader's trading account.

Additionally, the signal provider should post Forex Trading videos, webinars, and watch lists for additional customer support. Similarly, Forex Trading signal providers should be willing to answer all questions that pertain to trade formats and signals.

Should Forex Traders Use Free Forex Signals or Paid Forex Signals

Free forex signals and paid forex signals differ in terms of quality. Individuals who sell other products tend to issue out free forex signals. Therefore, although the individuals' free forex signals may work in getting a person interested in investing in Forex Trading training, the individuals have absolutely no interest in the quality of the signals themselves.

Additionally, free forex signal providers offer free trials that give beginners limited information that leaves the beginners wanting to learn more. Learning Forex Trading requires a lot of effort, which can yield positive outcomes. Consequently, even the best free Forex Trading signals do not teach beginners how to trade, because they cause the beginners to depend on other forex traders.

With paid forex signals, a person gets the experience he or she paid for. Paid forex signals give beginner traders access to support. For instance, when paid forex signals act unreliably, signal providers will provide the beginners with direction unlike using free forex signals where beginner traders will have no forthcoming support.

Therefore, a forex trader should not trust providers that guarantee results without proof. Genuine signal providers should be willing to share their performance history. Paid services provide helpful information for beginners to help them to become knowledgeable in forex money matters and the management of risks. Such data can be valuable to beginner traders who would like to control their investment directly in the future.

Forex Trading signals are instrumental in helping forex traders conduct market analysis within a short period. Similarly, forex signals mean that a trader will not have to sit down for extended hours waiting to get his or her outcomes. Moreover, forex traders can build their career within the first few months of their trading experience.

Chapter 8: Tips to Winning in Forex Trading

To the uninitiated, navigating the forex market successfully can seem like a difficult task. However, success is possible if one takes the right steps and trains properly. Just like training for a marathon, training is essential to winning in Forex Trading. Success requires targeted effort, practice, patience, and time.

Forex traders need to have specific goals in mind. With the right direction, training, and guidance, mastering the foreign exchange market is within anyone's reach. Winning at Forex Trading has little to do with hot picks, which are often fallacies created by people masquerading as experts in this field.

On the contrary, success stems from the ability to learn from both right and wrong trading choices to determine the patterns and strategies that work best for one's personality and goals. People are different; therefore, no single trading strategy will work for everyone.

Fortunately, there are several tips for winning in Forex Trading that can help beginners master the complexities of the largest market in the world. Actually, in terms of the value of average daily trading volume, the FX market dwarfs the bond and stock markets. Forex traders, therefore, have several inherent advantages over traders who engage in other forms of financial trading.

Small investors with modest capital can find success and trade their way to a fortune. The forex market is one of the few markets that can make this a reality. Trading the forex market is relatively easy. Doing it well and generating a consistent income, however, is not so easy. Therefore, it is important to learn the secrets and tips for success.

Tips and Secrets for Success in Forex Trading

1. Pay Attention to Daily Pivot Points

Forex traders should watch daily pivot points closely. This is especially important for day traders. However, it is also important for swing traders, position traders, and even traders who focus on long-term positions. It is important to do so because tons of other forex traders do the same.

In a certain way, pivot trading is like a self-fulfilling prophecy. Essentially, markets often find resistance or support at pivot points since thousands of pivot traders place orders at those points. Consequently, when a large volume of trading moves happens at these points or levels, there is no other reason for the move except that many traders placed orders expecting such a move.

However, pivot points should not be the only basis of a Forex Trading strategy. Rather, regardless of one's strategy, one should watch these points for signs of either potential market or continuation of a trend. Forex traders should look at pivot levels and the trading activities that take place around them as a confirming indicator to use in conjunction with their chosen strategy.

2. Define Trading Style and Goals

Before setting out on any journey, travelers need to have a clear idea of where they are going and how to get to their destination. In the same way, forex traders need to have clear goals, in addition to ensuring that their trading strategies will help them achieve those goals.

Each Forex Trading style or strategy comes with a different risk profile. Therefore, traders who want to win in Forex Trading need to find and adopt the right approach and attitude to trade profitably. Those who cannot imagine going to sleep with an open market position, for example, should consider focusing on day trading.

Forex traders with funds they believe will benefit from a trade appreciation over several months; on the other hand, they should think about position trading. Essentially, it is important for a forex trader to determine whether his/her personality will fit any particular trading strategy. Any mismatch will probably lead to certain losses and stress.

3. Trade with an Edge

Successful forex traders only risk their hard-earned money when a market opportunity provides them with an edge. In other words, they do so when the opportunity presents them with something that will boost the chances of their trades being successful. This edge can be various things, even a simple thing, such as selling at a price level that one identifies as strong resistance.

Forex traders can also increase their probability of success and their edge by having several technical factors in their favor. If the 100-period, 50-period, and 10-period moving averages all meet at the same price level, for example, it will likely offer significant resistance or support for a market because many traders will be acting together by trading off any of those averages.

Converging technical indicators also provide a similar edge. This happens when different indicators on many periods converge to provide resistance or support. Having the price hit an identified resistance or support level, in addition to having price movement at that level, is an indication of a potential market reversal.

4. The Trading Platform and Broker

Forex traders should spend adequate time researching a suitable trading platform and a reputable broker. It is important to identify and understand the difference between brokers and determine how each of them goes about making a market, as well as their policies. Trading the exchange-driven market, for example, is different from trading in the spot market or OTC market.

Traders should also choose the trading platform that fits the analysis they want to do. Traders who want to use Fibonacci numbers to trade, for example, should ensure the trading platform they choose has the ability to draw Fibonacci lives. A good platform with a bad broker is just as bad as a poor trading platform with a good broker. Therefore, forex traders need to find the best of both.

5. Preserve Capital

It is more important for traders to avoid huge losses than to make huge profits. For people who are new to Forex Trading, this concept may not sound quite right. However, it is important to understand that winning in Forex Trading means knowing how to preserve or protect one's capital.

According to the founder of Tudor Corporation, Paul Tudor Jones, playing great defense is the most important rule of trading. Actually, he is a great trader to learn from and study. In addition to building a hugely successful hedge fund, Tudor Jones has an excellent record of profitable trading.

He also played an important role in creating the ethics-training program needed to gain membership in all futures exchanges in the United States. Protecting the trading capital, or playing great defense, is very important in Forex Trading because many people who venture into Forex Trading are unable to continue trading as a result of running out of money.

Many forex traders drain their accounts soon after they make a few trades. Having strict risk management practices is important for people who want to win in Forex Trading. Traders who manage to preserve their trading capital are able to continue trading for as long as they want to, and might eventually become huge winners.

One great trade can fall into a trader's lap and significantly increase his/her profits and account size. One does not need to be the smartest trader in the world to make money in the forex market. If nothing else, the luck of the draw can have traders who manage to protect their capital stumble into trades that generate enough profits to make their trading careers a huge success.

6. Small Losses and Focus

After forex traders fund their trading accounts, they need to understand that their capital is at risk. Therefore, they should not depend on that money for their daily living expenses. Actually, it is better to think of those funds as vacation funds. Once their vacation is over, their money is gone.

Having this trading attitude will help prepare them to accept and learn from small losses, which will also help them manage their risk better. Forex traders should focus on their trades and accept small losses, which are normal in any type of business, rather than constantly and obsessively focusing on their equity.

7. Simple Technical Analysis

Consider this example of two forex traders in extremely different situations. The first trader has a specially designed trading computer with several monitors, a large office, swanky furnishings, trading charts, and market news feeds. He also has several moving averages, technical indicators, momentum indicators, and much more.

The other trader, on the other hand, works from a relatively simple office space and uses a regular desktop or laptop computer. His charts reveal just one or two technical indicators on the price action of the market.

Most people would consider the first trader to be more professional and extremely successful, and they would probably be wrong in their assumption. Actually, the second trader is closer to the image of a forex trader who wins consistently. Traders can apply numerous forms of technical analysis to a chart. Having more, however, does not necessarily mean having better.

Using a huge number of indicators might actually make things more complicated and confusing for a forex trader. They amplify indecision and doubt, causing him/her to miss many potentially profitable trades. Therefore, it is better to have a simple trading strategy with just a few rules, as well as a minimum of indicators to consider.

A few very successful forex traders make money from the forex market almost every day without using any technical indicators overlaid on their charts. They achieve this impressive feat without taking advantage of a relative strength indicator, trend lines, trading robots, moving averages, or expert advisors. Their market analysis involves a simple candlestick chart.

8. Weekend Analysis

The forex market ceases operation on the weekend. Therefore, forex traders should use this time to study their weekly charts to identify news or patterns that could affect their trades in either a positive or a negative way. This will give the objectivity, which will help them make smarter trading plans.

9. Placing Stop-Loss Orders at the Right Price Levels

In addition to protecting one's capital in case of a losing trade, this strategy is also an important aspect of smart Forex Trading. Many newcomers to the forex market assume that risk management simply means placing stop-loss orders close to the entry point of their trades. This is partly accurate; however, habitually placing stop-loss orders too close to their trade entry points is something that might contribute to their lack of success.

Sometimes, stop-loss orders can stop a trade, only to see the market make a reversal in favor of the trade. It is common for novice traders to endure watching this happen. Sometimes, this reversal proceeds to a level that would have seen them gain a sizable profit if the stop-loss order had not terminated the trade.

Obviously, traders should enter trades that allow them to place stop-loss orders close enough to their trade entry points to avoid making huge losses. However, they should place them at a reasonable price level, based on their analysis of the market. When it comes to reasonable placement of stop-loss orders, the general rule of thumb is to place them a bit further than the price the market should not trade at, based on market analysis.

10.   Use a Consistent Methodology

Before a prospective trader enters the forex market, he/she needs to have a good idea of how he/she will make trading decisions. Essentially, forex traders should know the information they will need to make smart decisions on entering a trade or exiting one. Some traders choose to analyze a chart and the fundamental of the economy to decide the best time to trade.

Others, however, prefer to perform technical analysis to determine the ideal time to execute a trade. Whichever methodology or strategy a trader chooses to employ, he/she needs to be consistent and ensure the chosen methodology is adequately adaptive. In other words, it should be flexible enough to handle the forex market's changing dynamics.

11.   Choosing the Right Entry and Exit Points

Most inexperienced forex traders do not know how to judge conflicting information that often presents when analyzing charts in various timeframes. Certain information, for example, might indicate a sell signal on a weekly chart, but show up as a purchasing opportunity in an intraday chart.

Therefore, if a trader is using a weekly chart to determine his/her basic trading direction and a daily chart to tie his/her entry, then he/she should try to synchronize the two charts. If the weekly chart is providing a buy signal, for example, he/she should wait for the daily chart to confirm this signal. In other words, keeping signal timing in sync is a good tip for winning in Forex Trading.

12.   Calculating Expectancy

The formula to use to determine the reliability of a trading system is expectancy. Forex traders should analyze and compare past winning trades against losing trades, which will help them determine the profitability of their winning trades versus how much money they lost in their losing trades.

A simple way to do this is by looking at their last 10 trades. New forex traders who have not yet made any trades should study their chart to identify points where their trading system suggests an entry and/or exit point. In other words, new forex traders need to determine whether their system is profitable.

Having done this, they should write down their observations, total their winning trades, and divide the amount by the number of successful trades they made. For example, if a trader made 10 trades, four of which flopped, and six of which were successful, his/her win ratio would be 60% or 6/10. If the six winning trades made $4,800, then his/her average win would be $4,800/6 = $800.

If the trader's losses amounted to $2,400, then his/her average loss would be $2,400/4 = $600. By applying these results to the formula for calculating the reliability of a system, the trader will get E = [1 + (800/600) x 0.6 – 1 = 0.4, which is equivalent to 40%. A positive expectancy of 40% means that the trader's trading system will likely generate 40 cents to the dollar over the long term.

13.　　　Positive Feedback Loops

Forex traders create a positive feedback loop following a well-planned and executed trade. When they plan a trade and execute it as expected, traders tend to create a pattern of positive feedback. In other words, success tends to breed success, which, in turn, builds confidence. This is especially true if the trade generates significant profits.

Even if a trader suffers a small loss following a well-planned trade, he/she will still build a positive feedback loop.

14.　　　Keeping Printed Records

Printed records serve as a good learning tool for forex traders. Therefore, traders, especially new ones, should print their charts create a list of reasons for any particular trade, including the things that sway their trading decisions. They should mark the entry and exit points on the chart and make any relevant comments, such as emotional reasons for taking specific actions.

Forex traders need to objectify their trades to develop the discipline and mental control needed to execute trades according to their systems, instead of their emotions, greed, or habits.

15.　　　Stress Less

This is an obvious Forex Trading tip. Trading the forex market under stress tends to lead to irrational decisions, which can end up costing a trader a lot of money. Therefore, forex traders should identify the source of their stress and try to get rid of it, or at least limit its influence on their actions.

When stress threatens to take control, a trader should take deep breaths and try to focus on other things for a few minutes. People have different ways of overcoming stress. Some exercise, while others listen to classical music. Traders should learn what works best for them.

Risk Management in Forex Trading

One of the most debated topics in financial trading is forex risk management. On one hand, forex traders want to get the most out of every trade, but on the other hand, they want to limit the size of a potential loss. Sometimes, traders need to take greater risks to gain the best returns. This is where the issue of risk management in Forex Trading arises.

Forex traders are in the business of making money. To do this, however, they need to learn how to limit potential losses. Unfortunately, many novice traders are just anxious to start trading without giving much thought to their total account size. They do not think of ways to minimize their potential losses before hitting the 'trade' button.

This type of investing is more akin to gambling. When forex traders make trades without following the rules of risk management, they are, in fact, gambling. They are hoping to land that jackpot, instead of focusing on the long-term returns on their investment. Risk management rules do not offer 100% protection; however, they can make traders very profitable in the end.

Consider this; people go to Las Vegas every day to gamble in hopes of winning a jackpot. Some do win; however, casinos still make tons of money. If people are winning big jackpots, how are casinos making so much money in the end? The answer is that they are still profitable because they earn more money from losing gamblers.

Casinos are excellent statisticians. They know that numerous gamblers will lose, and their money will be more than enough to pay for the jackpots won by the few successful gamblers. This is a good example of how casinos know how to control their losses. In the same way, forex traders need to know how to control their losses to improve their chances of being profitable.

Forex Trading, in the end, is a numbers game, which means that traders have to tilt every factor in their favor. Essentially, they need to be the statistician and not the gambler. Everyone knows that it takes money to make money. The money one needs to start trading largely depends on one's approach to a new trading business.

Losses are a reality of business, and traders will suffer some losses at some point in their career. This is the reason why it is important to have some risk management rules. Forex traders should only risk a small percentage of their accounts on each trade so that they can survive losses and avoid large drawdowns in their accounts.

New forex traders tend to assume that making money through Forex Trading is easy and fast. To find success in this business, however, traders need patience, commitment, dedication, and time. Traders should not just open trading positions without considering the currency risk, trading conditions, and risks that can affect their invested capital.

They need to use techniques and tools to manage their investments and risks. Those who fail to do this will be gambling instead of trading. Some of the best ways to manage risks in Forex Trading include:

1. Only Investing Money, one Does not Need

The first rule in any form of trading, including Forex Trading, is to invest the money one can afford to lose. Most beginners tend to skip or ignore this rule since they assume that it will not happen to them. Even gamblers do not take all their money to the casino to bet on black. Forex traders should not take unnecessary risks by investing the money they need.

Trading with money they need for their daily living expenses will only add emotional stress and extra pressure on their trading, which will affect their decision-making abilities and increase the likelihood of making costly mistakes. In addition, there is a chance they could lose all their trading capital.

The FX market is an unpredictable and volatile market; therefore, it is safer to trade conservative amounts from one's disposable income.

2. Think About Risk Tolerance

Before traders start trading, they need to identify and understand their risk tolerance, which will depend on the following:

1. Investment goals
2. Their age

3. How much they are willing to lose

4. Their experience

5. Their knowledge of the foreign exchange market

By determining their risk tolerance, forex traders will know they are in control of any situation because they are risking the right amount of money in terms of their financial objectives in relation to their personal financial situation.

3. Set Risk to Reward Ratio (RRR) to a Minimum of 1:3

Having a good understanding of the RR ratio will improve a trader's chances of being profitable, in addition to setting limit orders to protect his/her trading capital. The RR ratio compares and measures the distance between a trader's entry point and his/her take-profit and stop-loss orders.

For example, suppose that a trader is investing in the EUR/USD currency pair. If 50 pips is the distance between his/her entry point and stop-loss point, and 150 pips between the entry point and take-profit point, then he/she would be using a risk/reward ratio of 50:150, which is 1:3 because he/she is risking 50 pips to gain 150 pips.

The risk to reward ratio is an important tool to help traders set their take-profit and stop-loss orders, depending on their risk tolerance. Smart forex traders should control their downside risk. Although the RRR depends on a trader's risk tolerance, most traders use a ratio of 1:3, which means that they hope to earn 3 times what they are willing to lose.

4. Control the Risk per Trade

When thinking about their trading risks, forex traders should consider their trading capital. A smart risk management strategy would be to invest a small percentage of their trading capital in each trade. For example, 1% to 2% of their available capital per trade is a good starting point.

If a forex trader has $10,000 in his/her trading account, for example, the maximum loss allowable would be 2% of the available capital, which will amount to $200 per trade. Controlling the risk per trade is very helpful, especially if a trader goes through a losing streak. It helps forex traders to avoid huge drawdowns in their trading accounts and protect their trading capital.

5. Keep the Risk Consistent

As soon as they make their first profits, some forex traders, especially beginners, increase the size of their positions, which is a good way to wipe out their trading accounts. Forex traders should understand the importance of keeping their trading risk consistent. Just because a trader is on a winning streak does not mean that the next trade will make a profit.

Traders should avoid becoming risk-averse and over-confident since it can lead to them to change their risk and money management rules without good reasons. When they were working on their trading strategies, they probably set up rules to guide their trading positions. This is a necessary step towards setting up a winning trading strategy; however, they also need to stick to their rules to achieve long-term success.

6. Understand and Control Leverage

Due to its high volatility, the FX market is a leveraged market. In this case, leverage refers to the ability to invest more than the initial deposit through margin trading. Forex brokers will only ash traders to set aside a small amount of the total value of their positions as collateral.

By using leverage, traders can increase their profits quickly; however, they need to understand that this also applies to their losses. Therefore, they need to understand how margin trading and leverage work, in addition to how they affect their overall trading and performance.

However, using high leverage to generate huge profits, as some inexperienced traders do, is not a good idea. This is because a small change in the market can easily wipe out their trading accounts. In fact, the European Securities and Market Authority set limitations on the leverage brokers offer in August 2018.

7. Consider Currency Correlations

Since forex traders trade currency pairs, such as EUR/USD, it is important to understand the correlation between currencies linked to each other. Having a good understanding of currency correlations will help them control their trading portfolios more effectively by reducing the overall risk.

Correlation describes how one currency behaves in relation to another currency. When two currencies have a positive correlation, it means that they usually move in the same direction. Those with a negative correlation, on the other hand, will move in opposite directions.

To use currency correlations to their advantage, traders need to understand a few important things:

a) They should avoid opening several trading positions that conflict or cancel out each other

b) They should have a good understanding of commodity currencies

c) They should avoid opening trading positions with the same quote currency or base currency

No matter how unrealistic it may sound, many people going into Forex Trading expect to get rich overnight. The world of FX trading can be complicated and overwhelming, especially for beginners who do not know the rules. Before people go any deeper, they need to dip their toes into the forex pool.

Chapter 9: Cryptocurrency in Forex Trading

A cryptocurrency is a digital currency that acts as a medium of exchange. Currencies have gone through a series of changes since the barter system in the Stone Age period, to the paper currency in later years.

The term 'crypto' in cryptocurrency comes from the word 'cryptography.' Cryptography is a technique of using encryption and decryption as a means to safeguard communication in the company of third parties with ill motives. In order to work, cryptography requires a computational algorithm, a public key that the trader shares with everybody, and a private key, which acts like the trader's digital signature, which the trader keeps secret.

In Forex Trading, forex traders use cryptocurrencies as modes of payments and as trading instruments, forming currency pairs with other cryptocurrencies and currencies.

At this point, the future of currency could be cryptocurrencies. There are two major cryptocurrencies in the market: the bitcoin and ether. The bitcoin is a type of digital currency that is independent of a central authority. That is, the central bank does not regulate the distribution of bitcoins in the market. Instead, bitcoin uses a blockchain to carry out transactions on a peer-to-peer network.

Bitcoins started circulating in 2009, and its success has generated several competing cryptocurrencies called 'altcoins' or alternative coins. Altcoins include Litecoin (LTC), Namecoin, Peercoin (PPCoin), Ripple, EOS, and Cardano, among thousands of other cryptocurrencies currently in existence.

Ether is a type of currency that the Ethereum network acknowledges. Ethereum runs on blockchain technology to establish an open-source platform to create and redistribute applications that are decentralized, or independent of central authority.

Bitcoin and ether are the most significant and most valuable cryptocurrencies in the international market. While bitcoins transactions are manual, ether transactions can be both manual and automatic. A trader can use bitcoins for transactions involving goods and services, whereas ether uses blockchain to create ledgers that activate operations once a trader meets the required conditions.

Litecoin is similar to bitcoin in that Litecoin relies on an open-source global payment network that is not under any central authority's regulation. However, Litecoin has a more rapid block generation rate compared to bitcoin, since Litecoin uses a different algorithm.

Namecoin is more of an experimental open-source technology that boosts security, independence from a central regulating authority, censorship resistance, speed of internet infrastructure such as the Domain Name System (DNS), and privacy. Traders can use Namecoin to record and transfer random keys or names in a safeguarded manner. It also has the ability to attach data to the random names. In that regard, Namecoin offers advanced privacy competences.

Peercoin (PPCoin) is one of the leading forms of cryptocurrencies with regard to market capitalization. It is the first digital currency that employs a combination of proof-of-work and proof-of-stake. The proof-of-stake algorithm formulates from the coins that individual traders hold. A trader holding 2% of the currency should receive a reward of 2% of all proof-of-stake coin blocks.

The proof-of-work blocks are less rewarding because the portion of the proof-of-work algorithm requires intensive energy for generating blocks compared to the minimal energy the proof-of-stake algorithm uses to create blocks. Consequently, the Peercoin network will become more energy-efficient as proof-of-stake rewards do not need a lot of processing power.

Ripple is both a cryptocurrency and a payment system. With regard to Ripple's cryptocurrency aspect, it follows an algorithm like every other cryptocurrency. Ripple's payment system makes it possible for users to transfer money in any currency to another user on the Ripple network in a matter of seconds. That means that Ripple transactions are much faster than other crypto coins, including bitcoin.

EOS is a robust infrastructure for decentralized applications that is blockchain-based and facilitates the development hosting and performance of economic-scale decentralized applications (dApps) on its platform. EOS uses the proof-of-stake idea to make instant high-level decisions among designated stakeholders.

Cardano is both a cryptocurrency and a decentralized platform that authorizes transactions without high-energy costs. Cardano seeks to safeguard the privacy of traders while being regulator-friendly.

The platform uses the Ouroboros Pos algorithm to authenticate transactions.

Why use cryptocurrencies?

Little to No Operation Costs: When traders use traditional ways of carrying out transactions using paper currencies, they lose some amount of money when transferring currencies to or from bank accounts.

Cryptocurrencies have the lowest transaction fees, which amount to only about $2. An individual may encounter only three transaction fees. The charges include the exchange fees, the network fees, and the digital wallet fees when a person wants to store his or her crypto coins in the digital wallet.

24/7 Access to Money: Unlike using banks, individuals can access cryptocurrencies anytime, any day. Given that cryptocurrencies are not subject to any central authority, an individual can have access to the crypto coins any time of the day, even in the middle of the night.

Similarly, an individual can make unlimited purchases and withdrawals. That is contrary to using bank services where the bank places limits on the amount of money an individual can spend within 24-hours.

Available for Anyone: Billions of people around the world do not have access to bank accounts. However, many people have access to mobile phones and can use cryptocurrencies and blockchain technology to execute financial transactions through biometric, thus promoting prosperity.

Additionally, the process of signing up to use cryptocurrencies is brief and requires no paperwork.

Fast International Transactions: Unlike in banks, where transferring money from one place to another can take hours, transferring cryptocurrencies is a matter of seconds. That is because when moving cryptocurrency from one place to another, transactions do not need to go through all of the same checks and balances processes that banks follow before depositing funds.

Cryptocurrency transfers, whether within a country or outside the country, are quick and instant and do not require any transaction costs. Additionally, individuals can track their transactions in the blockchain.

High Privacy Levels: With cryptocurrencies, an individual does not have to provide personal information. That is contrary to banks, where individuals have to provide extensive personal data.

Moreover, individuals can carry out safe transactions because of the encryptions that go into the code of cryptocurrencies. Therefore, traders can have confidence in the cryptocurrencies security guarantee as more people use the specific blockchain.

People Have Control Over Their Own Money: Cryptocurrencies are not subject to the rules and regulations that the banks and other financial institutions enforce. If an individual remembers the password or the passphrase of his or her digital wallet, the cryptocurrencies are entirely under the control of the individual, and no one else can have access to the crypto coins.

Cryptocurrencies allow individuals to carry out trade with other people independently, without the presence of a third party or bank interference. That is because transactions with cryptocurrencies are peer-to-peer, meaning from people to people.

Reliable Alternative to Unstable Currencies: Cryptocurrencies does not bring about inflation and economic instability that individuals often experience from using traditional paper currencies. While not all individuals are subject to the incredible rates of inflation, other individuals can benefit greatly from shifting to use cryptocurrencies.

Many countries around the world allow the use of cryptocurrency, which is not affected by forex rates and interest rates. In fact, cryptocurrency offers more solidity and assurance to people living in economically unstable countries.

Accountability of Individuals and Companies: Regrettably, there are several business entities and big industries out in the business world, which allow corrupt and illegal business tendencies. Individuals want to ensure that they carry out their trades with honesty and integrity, upholding the trading rights and following the rules of conduct. However, trusting that a company or an individual has integrity based on the information they provide about themselves is not a reliable way to know the morals of their real practices.

Luckily, cryptocurrency introduces the blockchain technology that will change the way individuals and companies practice a trade — blockchain technology, which is not subject to change, unlike the traditional paper currency. Cryptocurrencies and blockchain technologies make companies and individuals answerable to clients. Moreover, traders get the opportunity to know more about the companies they trade with.

Strengthen E-Commerce: Given that many people like to carry out most of their transactions online nowadays, cryptocurrencies provide a safe option for shoppers to buy as many things as they would want, without concerns for fraud.

Cryptocurrencies not only reduce the risk of fraud for online shoppers, but they also protect the business vendors and merchandisers. Cryptocurrency transactions are permanent. That is because the cryptocurrency's electronic network ledger records the transactions. As a result, the transactions become irreversible and unchangeable, thus mitigating risk.

Additionally, using cryptocurrency creates endless opportunities for global commerce.

Secure Handling of Smart Contracts: Blockchain technology enables individuals to computerize practically every physical object or service in the blockchain. For example, when selling property, an individual can enter the value of the property into the blockchain and sell the property through automatic or smart contracts.

Consequently, banks, notaries, and financial advisors will no longer be necessary because individuals are able to carry out trades in faster and inexpensive ways. Additionally, an individual can securely manage his or her personal information in the blockchain and use it for taking loans, insurances, or even purchasing travel tickets.

Governments can also use automatic or smart contracts when giving out permits, when holding elections, and when collecting taxes, among other government tasks. Blockchain technology will also ensure transparency in government operations.

What are the disadvantages of using cryptocurrencies?

To begin with, cryptocurrency is a concept that is difficult to understand. People who are not tech-savvy may not understand how the blockchains work, or how blockchains store cryptocurrencies. In that regard, individuals are cautious of taking advantage of the benefits that cryptocurrency can offer.

As such, most people do not know the benefits of using cryptocurrency. However, it appears that, that more and more people are acquiring information about the digital currency. The response, therefore, is slow because people are not yet ready to make the switch from using banks to using cryptocurrency.

As more individuals enter into the cryptocurrency domain by acquiring their crypto every day, there is still a long way to go and a lot of work to do with regard to the teaching people how cryptocurrencies work. Consequently, a cryptocurrency needs to circulate the money market more, so that people can have exposure to it and they can begin to accept to use it

The other significant drawback that cryptocurrencies have is the challenge of constant fluctuations in their market prices. As a result, traders find it challenging to use the crypto because traders can never be entirely sure what the value of the crypto will be in the upcoming days.

Additionally, most traders do not accept digital money. That is because the concept of digital money is still new, and many traders do not trust digital money yet. What's more, many companies have not embraced the use of digital funds, even though cryptocurrency is a growing trend. The reason for that could be that companies are not willing to take a risk with the constantly changing prices. In addition, companies may not be aware of how cryptocurrency can generate profits.

Lastly, most people may not know where to get cryptocurrencies, how to store, and how to use the cryptos. Although people can search for information on cryptos online, the idea is that no person, young and old, should have any challenges when it comes to dealing with cryptocurrencies. Instead, the trade should become an organic or natural part of people's lives, the same way that paper currency is.

In conclusion, the rate at which the world is becoming technologically interconnected calls for a complete transformation in the process of buying and selling products and services. Cryptocurrencies are one of the ground-breaking innovations in the context of technological interconnectedness that will revolutionize global forex trade.

Consequently, more traders will accept cryptocurrencies, and more people will switch to using cryptos. In that way, cryptocurrencies have a huge potential to become the most widely used medium of exchange in the future.

Chapter 10: Examples of Trade

Forex trade involves a trader going long for the first currency and short for the second one. He or she purchases the first currency using money and then waits before selling it to make a profit. The trade takes place utilizing the current rates of exchange at the time of the transaction. Thus, the fluctuations in the exchange rates determine if the value of a particular currency is high or low. It helps a trader decide when to enter or exit a trade, or when to buy or sell a currency.

For example, a trader followed the prevailing GBP/USD exchange rates and paid USD 24,200 to purchase GBP 20,000 in mid-January 2017. The value of the British pound increased over the following months against the dollar. The trader then decided to sell the £20,000 that he has for approximately $27,000. He or she closed out his or her position and received USD 27,000. Thus, he or she made a profit of USD 2,800 because initially, he or she started with USD 24,200 and closed out with USD 27,000.

A trader can utilize various strategies and means to ensure that he or she achieves success in Forex Trading. He or she can use trading instruments such as disposable risks, leveraged features, spread bets, and CDF contracts. A CDF contract is a deal between two sides to trade the difference between the closing price and opening price of a contract. It stands for 'Contract for difference' and is a complicated, advanced, and high-risk instrument as a trader can experience a rapid loss due to leveraged features.

The following are some examples of forex trade and the outcomes that indicate a winning or losing trade:

Example 1

A trader can calculate his or her profits and losses when he or she closes out a forex trade. He or she finds the difference between the price of buying and selling the currency and multiplies it by the transaction size. The difference will determine whether he or she experiences a winning or a losing trade. For instance, a trader purchases Euros (EUR/USD) at 1.2166 and later sells them at 1.2156. The transaction size of that trade is 100,000 Euros. He or she will calculate the profit using the formula: ($1.2166 - $1.2156) × 100,000. This will lead to $0.001 × 100,000 = $100. Hence, his or her profit from that forex trade will be $100.

Likewise, the forex trader will calculate a loss if he or she sold the Euros (EUR/USD) at 1.2060 and buy them at 1.2070. He or she will use the formula ($1.2060 - $1.2070) × 100,000. This will give -$0.001 × 100,000 = -$100. Thus, he or she will have a loss of $100 from that trade.

Moreover, the trader can use the current bid to find out his or her unrealized losses and profits on open positions. He or she substitutes that bid accordingly in the formula to calculate the unrealized profit or loss. For example, if he or she purchased Euros at 1.2166, and the current rate of a bid is 1.2116, then his or her unrealized loss is $50. The calculation is ($1.2161 - $1.2166) × 100,000= -$0.0005 × 100,000 = $50. If he or she sold the Euros at 1.2060 and the current bid rate is 1.2055, the unrealized profit here is $50: ($1.2060 - $1.2055) × 100,000= $0.0005 × 100,000= $50.

The trader subtracts any extra charges in the transactions like commissions, to find out his or her exact profits and losses.

Example 2

A trader can transact in the forex market in terms of the amount of money he or she is willing to risk. He or she takes a certain amount from his or her investments fund account and uses it to trade. He or she can win and double the initial risked amount or not succeed and end up losing the money. For instance, a trader has $10,000 in his or her account as the money available as a disposable risk. During an investment, he or she decides to use $2,000 and ventures that amount in the forex trade.

The trader researches and finds out that the chances of achieving a profit goal of interest are 70%. He or she can then choose to invest that amount in the trade in two ways. First, he or she can risk the entire $2,000 and form a profit goal of $2,000 while going long at the opening. Additionally, he or she can also set a stop loss of $2,000 in the trade. If the deal succeeds, he or she wins an additional $2,000 in profits. Nonetheless, he or she may also lose the business, and the entire invested amount since the risk of failing, in this case, is at 30%.

The second way that the trader can invest the money is to split it and risk only $200 per trade. He or she also modifies the profit goal to $200. Thus, he or she can make ten trades and significantly reduce the chances of losing the entire $2,000 since the risk associated here is less than 1%.

Example 3

A forex trader can also use a leveraged instrument to trade, which provides him or her with a trading margin. He or she makes a profit if the trade moves in his or her direction margin. Conversely, he or she loses the deal if it pushes against the trader. For instance, a trader with an investment amount of $6,000 trades on a margin of 1:50. This margin means that he or she can practically manage a capital of $300,000.

A beginning trader utilizes a smaller margin of 1:20 to minimize the risks associated with contrasting trade moves that can result in a 100% loss of capital. Thus, he or she uses a margin of 1:20 with the initial money of $6,000, which enables him or her to control $120,000. He or she decides to bet that the USD will fall against the Euro and then enters a trade on a long side to transact the EUR/USD. The current exchange rate of the EUR/USD is 1.405, while he or she will practically be trading $120,000 to Euros. He or she calculates it by the 120,000/1.405 = 71,174 Euros.

Forex Trading involves several strategies that a trader can employ in the market. He or she can study the various ways of Forex Trading and select the ones that best suit his or her profit goal and trading tactics.

Chapter 11: Mistake That Beginners Make in Forex Trading

All traders have passed through the beginners' phase, and they have made their share of newbie mistakes. Most traders continue to make mistakes as they venture deep into trading, but smart ones view these mistakes as learning opportunities rather than sulk over then. People can be very emotional where their money is concerned, but it is important for traders to detach themselves from this mindset so that they can make rational decisions.

The occasional lapse is forgivable, but at the end of it all, the trader's money is at stake, so he or she should work hard to protect it and grow it. If you are new to trading, you can learn from those who have gone ahead of you and avoid some of the common mistakes that they have made which include:

1. Trading Without Much Knowledge

The first mistake that people make when they decide to try Forex Trading is getting into the forex market without proper knowledge of how to maneuver and make money. Forex Trading is something that takes years to master. In addition to trading knowledge, experts in trading have vast experience in trading. Although newbies might have the former and not the latter, they can still succeed in trading but with proper planning and guidance.

Investing in the forex market is similar to investing in a business. People hardly invest in sectors or businesses that they have little knowledge. They usually take their time to study how to conduct business in a particular area. People interested in Forex Trading should also treat trading as a business that they are interested in investing in. They should not forget that they need to protect their capital just as they would if they were putting it in a business venture by stocking up on information.

New traders can gather information from trading books, articles, and any other material available that touches on the subject. There are also people who offer classes in the form of webinars and seminars. Beginners can also practice with demo accounts. Successful traders are well informed; they know the markets they operate in as well as indicators and strategies for investing in the stock market.

2. Trading Without a Plan

Trading plans are very crucial in investing in the financial markets. They offer a trader with a guideline of how they will invest their money in the forex market. More specifically, they detail the amount of money a trader is willing to put in a trade, the market conditions that are favorable for a person to trade, the duration of stay in the market and the exact time to get out of the market either after experiencing a loss or even after making a profit. Without such guidelines, traders conduct their business blindly with no focus.

Many new beginners in Forex Trading are guilty of this mistake. They enter the forex market without any plan and wonder why they keep failing in the trade. New beginners can formulate trading plans then test them in a demo account. They can keep adjusting their plans as they see fit until they are ready to test in the real market.

Once a trader begins to use his plan, he should ensure that he follows it. This way, he is able to remain rational when trading and keep his emotions at bay. The stop loss and stop profit serve to guide the trader on when to exit the market to avoid losing money and when a trade has been exhausted. More importantly, as traders write down their plans, they should focus on the right goals. If chasing after huge profits are all a trader wants, then he or she is bound to get disappointed. Setting realistic goals is crucial, even if it means making a little consistent profit.

3. Lack of Money Management

New traders are at free will to decide how much they are willing to invest in a trade. However, a number of beginners overleverage their capital. They put money that they cannot afford to lose in a single trade and risk a huge percentage of their portfolio or investment in the trade. Since making profits is never guaranteed, there is always the risk of losing money or the entire investment if one is not careful about how they manage their money.

New traders should calculate how much money they are willing to risk in a single trade according to their risk appetite. They should not make some decisions on a whim. The best way is to have a guideline from the beginning, in the form of a trading plan. A trader should know how many trades he or she should enter at any one single time. Without understanding, his or her risk/reward ratio, or win/loss ratio, a trader can end up investing his or her capital in the wrong way and lose the entire investment.

Therefore, it is crucial that traders and especially the new ones to learn a few money management skills before they join the market; otherwise, they may not survive in trading.

4. Overtrading

Some new traders are very fond of overtrading. This can mean that they either trade with money that they do not have or risk a big portion of their investment in a single trade. Insufficient capitalization is dangerous and is ill-advised. Traders should only trade with money that they have and not money that does not exist or money they have borrowed.

It is always devastating for a trader to lose money that they did not have. This often leads to them borrowing money elsewhere to compensate for their loss, or they have to struggle to get back above the margins. Even when a trader begins to make money, they should have a guideline of how much of their profit they should reinvest back in the market and how much of their capital they should put back.

Another mistake new beginner is fond of making is trading when the markets are not favorable as stipulated in their trading plan. When traders deviate from their plans and get into markets that they should not, then it means that they are overtrading. New traders should not assume that their strategies are faulty when the markets do not favor even if it is for a long while. Instead of getting into shaky water, new traders should always choose to save their money over spending it then losing some of it.

5. Trading Without a Stop Loss

A stop loss is very important as it acts as a warning sign to a trader and tells him or her when to stop trading because of the risk of losing further amounts with an investment. Due to possibly a lack of experience, some beginners never know when to cut their losses and move on to the next trade. When they start losing money, they always think that they can recover their money, so they continue trading despite their margins running out.

Other traders may have stop losses, but they do not have the discipline to stick to them. This group is no different from the one without a stop loss. Another set of traders may be tempted to move their stop loss in the negatives or readjust it to accommodate more losses when they trade, but this is also ill-advised. Traders should always move stop losses upwards and in the direction of a win rather than down and to an even larger loss position.

6. Ignoring News and Market Trends

New traders should also stick to their plans when they venture or approach trading markets. However, their plans should be flexible to accommodate market conditions as well as any news or events that might affect the movement of the market. For example, a trader might spot a good USD to EUR exchange. However, something might happen in Europe that might blow up the deal without the trader's knowledge. Without this information, from let us say the balance trade report from Europe, a trader cannot make an informed decision. Traders are supposed to make event calendars as they catch up with their daily news, this way, they are able to monitor and keep in mind what could affect their future trading decisions as well as any curveballs that they might encounter. Various tools can assist traders to check on prevailing ranges and trends. Understanding the history of a certain market can also help a trader know what the future market might look like.

7. Trading with Emotions

Trading with emotions or gut feelings is very common with all traders, not just new ones. Rather than use hunches, traders should study markets and read the statistics in order to make rational decisions. When the market seems to be favorable, it is very easy for a trader to put in more money or stay for a bit longer.

This is risky because trading markets can sometimes be volatile; they can change in an instant or overnight, leaving a trader in regret. It is important for beginners to stick to their trading plan. They should know when to collect their profit bags and leave. Similarly, when a new trader encounters a loss, they also take a break from the market but not a long one. Refraining from trading or sulking over previous losses is emotional trading. Even expert traders make losses and mistakes, but they always choose to pick up the pieces and move on to another trader rather than seat down and sulk.

If a trader is also too cautious, they can miss great deals that are within their trading plans. This fear can also make a trader deviate from his or her plan and try out trades that are not within the plan. This decision has the potential to lead to even further losses. In most cases, a good trading plan can recover losses. If this does not happen, then the trader can pull away from the forex market, assess their plan, or look for the problem in their plan, then adjust accordingly and get back into the game.

8. Adding to a Losing Trade

Sometimes beginners in trading are tempted to continue adding to an unprofitable trade, but eventually, even they can attest that this is a wrong move. No matter how sure a trader is about the next move in the market, multiplying losses is never a good idea. In most cases, it leaves the trader in a deeper loss position. Most traders in this situation are also incapable of making unbiased decisions that are within their trading plans. It is always better for the trader to close with a negative position than to increase their loss. It is okay to step back and regroup. The trader can also try another trade or wait for the market to be favorable again.

As earlier deduced, it is never a good idea to move the stop loss in an effort to avoid closing at a loss. New traders must learn the discipline of sticking to their plans and observing any guidelines that they had set before entering the market. Traders should also refrain from revenging on the market. Revenge trades can even make a trader double or triple the current loss that they have.

9. Choosing the Wrong Broker

The first and probably the most critical decision for a new trader is choosing a good broker. Giving money to another person is the first and biggest gamble that a trader will ever make. Whichever company the trader decides to give his or her trading capital should be legit. There have been incidents of people giving away their money to scammers.

A good broker should allow a trader to trade freely with his or her money and withdraw it whenever he or she wishes to do so. The first step in choosing the right broker is to look for one that matches your needs. If you have a small amount of capital, you should look at brokers who allow trading in micro-lots. The broker should also be regulated in the country they operate in and have a stable financial system.

It is important to carry a background check on the broker by researching on reviews about the broker. A trader should also check whether a broker allows them to deal directly with the market, or they normally redirect them to a dealing desk. He should also look at the willingness of the broker to address his concerns. Once the trader is okay with the above, he can open a demo account to test whether the broker offers what they say they offer. Smart traders do not deposit their entire trading capital with a broker; instead, they test the water first to assess the broker's availability, support, and accessibility to their money. If a broker proves worthy, a trader can go ahead and deposit the rest of his money.

Chapter 12: How to Make Money with Forex Trading to Create Passive Income

According to experts in the field of Forex Trading, it is possible to create a passive income through this form of financial trading. However, before jumping headlong into this type of financial trading, prospective traders need to ask themselves whether it is suitable for them, in addition to learning as much as possible about this line of business.

A passive income is the income stream traders or investors get at regular intervals and require little or no effort on their part to maintain it. Some of the common types of passive income include dividends from stock owned in a listed corporation, rental income, and interest income from bonds.

Other less common forms of passive income include royalties from a music record or publishing a book, or dividends from a non-listed company run by a family member or friend. Passive income may also arise from a new business model or income from a multi-level marketing network, where the income originates from other people's activities.

Some internet marketers, such as affiliate marketers, also receive passive income from internet traffic that continues to stream in from blogs they posted a long time ago. Nowadays, traders can make a passive income through the forex market.

In fact, one does not have to participate directly in the trading process or have tons of experience in this field of business. Forex traders can earn a passive income from this form of financial trading in several ways, with some requiring more work or input from the trader. Some of these include:

Forex Signals

These are short messages new traders can use to determine the best currency to trade and the right time to trade. Traders can receive important trading information through email, text messages, or any other type of communication, including social media platforms such as TX forums, Twitter, and other leading financial trading platforms.

These signals or messages are usually brief snippets of information, which instruct users to take specific actions, such as purchasing EUR/USD at a certain price. Sometimes, these signals feature various types of orders, such as a market order, pending order, or limit order. There are tons of sites that teach traders how to read and understand forex signals.

These signals can also be premium or free, with the former leading to better trades. Many providers of forex signals freely send important trading information to investors to boost their reputation in the financial trading industry. Forex signals are also great for people who want to earn a passive income trading options but do not have the time or opportunity to learn much about Forex Trading.

However, it is important to perform adequate research into providers of forex signals to avoid losing money. Forex traders, however, should approach these signals with utmost caution to make a good passive income.

Forex Robots

One of the best ways to make a passive income from the forex market is using a tool known as a forex robot, which performs automated trades on a trader's behalf. Once traders set up these forex robots, they do not have to do much else; however, they should keep an eye on the trades the forex robots are making for them.

To get started, traders need to perform adequate research into the software available for forex robots. They need to choose software that will meet their needs, in addition to being reliable when it comes to executing the right forex trades. After setting up this software, it will make forex trades based on preset signals.

In addition, it will use its acquired knowledge to purchase or sell at specific times, earning users a passive income in the process. However, it is important to understand that not all forex robots make passive income for investors as claimed. In the same way that a human can make a losing trade, a forex robot can also make the same mistake.

It is also important to understand that many so-called forex robots are frauds, which is why respected news platforms such as the Wall Street Journal and Forbes refuse to promote or advertise them. Unfortunately, this is particularly true when it comes to free forex robots. Therefore, new forex traders should analyze testimonials and reviews carefully before entrusting their investment to a forex robot.

Fortunately, several leading sites focus on reviewing different trading platforms. These sites try to give an honest opinion of different investment platforms and outline all the benefits and limitations of each platform. They also offer a detailed analysis of how these platforms work and how traders can get started on them, which is especially helpful to new traders.

Social Trading

The social trading network works in the same way as a social networking platform. Instead of sharing selfies or pictures of pets playing the piano, however, social traders share important information about forex or financial trades. This allows others to copy them and make passive income as well.

New forex traders simply need experienced traders they trust and copy their trading strategies to make money. In addition to making a passive income, they will also learn when, why, and how successful traders make their trading moves, which will give them more insight and understanding into the forex industry.

However, finding traders, they can trust and emulate is not as easy as it may sound. New traders need to set aside adequate time to perform thorough research into different social trading platforms, in addition to learning more about forex traders they want to work with and copy.

In certain situations, they might need to spend some money on the trader whose trading strategies they copy. However, this commission is negligible and not a big concern for new traders who want to make a passive income. Forex Trading is something that most people looking for ways to make some extra cash look into.

However, most of them do not know where to start. This discussion provides three great ideas for Forex Trading beginners to consider. Each of the options above requires a different investment in terms of time and effort. The most important thing to remember is that beginners should perform adequate research before picking a trading platform or strategy to use.

Nowadays, Forex Trading is one of the best ways for people to make a passive income working online. Millions of traders are earning a passive or active income every day through Forex Trading. This line of business is just like any other online money-making concept, but its profit potential is unrivaled. With modern technological advances and the availability of detailed information, anyone can make a passive income through Forex Trading.

Conclusion

Thank you for making it through to the end of *Forex Trading for Beginners: Simple Strategies to Make Money with Forex Trading: The Best Guide with Basics, Secrets Tactics, and Psychology to Big Profit and Income from the Financial Market.* Let us hope it was informative and able to provide you with all of the tools you need to achieve your goals, whatever they may be.

Now you know that the word 'forex' is short for 'foreign exchange,' and it involves converting one currency into another for reasons including tourism, trading, and business. The foreign exchange market is a global forum for exchanging substantial national currencies against each other.

The foreign exchange market is open to all types of traders, and it is more accessible than any other online trading platform in the world. An individual can start trading with as little as $100. Therefore, foreign exchange markets have lower exchange capital prerequisites compared to other financial markets.

Forex Trading happens over the interbank market, which is a channel through which currency trading happens 5 days a week, 24 hours a day. It is one of the biggest trading markets in the world, with a worldwide daily turnover estimated to be more than $5 trillion.

If the currency pair of EUR/USD, which refers to Euro/US Dollar, was trading at 1.0914/1.0916, for example, investors planning to open a long position on the Euro would purchase one Euro for

1.0916 US dollars. They will then hold on to the currency and hope that its value will increase, and then sell it back to the market once it appreciates. On the other hand, investors looking to open a short position on the Euro will sell one Euro for 1.0914 US dollars, with the expectation that its value will depreciate. If their expectations come true, they will buy it back at the lower rate and make a profit.

Brokers are the intermediaries who link investors with their capital. Some traders may choose to invest in the forex trade, and therefore they will invariably become in need of a foreign exchange broker.

The account balance is the amount of equity or capital available in your brokerage account due to investment in the currency market. It is essential to have such an account to enable the foreign exchange broker to carry out the buying and selling executions on your behalf.

A Forex Trading platform is a standard provision from most forex brokers to their clients, investors, or other retail traders. It also acts as a source of commission for the forex brokers by charging an access fee to use it. After seeking a foreign exchange broker, most traders will get a couple of trading platform recommendations from these same brokers.

Forex Trading signals are guidelines and recommendations that help inexperienced forex traders to open Forex Trading positions. The signals are a type of system that forex traders use to make crucial decisions about their trade. In that regard, Forex Trading signals provide details about how to open a new Forex Trade.

To the uninitiated, navigating the forex market successfully can seem like a difficult task. However, success is possible if one takes the right steps and trains properly. Just like training for a marathon, training is essential to winning in Forex Trading. Success requires targeted effort, practice, patience, and time.

Your next step should be to get a Forex Trading account, implement the strategies within the pages of this book, and start smiling all the way to the bank.

Finally, if you found this book useful in any way, a review on Amazon is always appreciated!

9 781802 909470